Copyright © 2019 All rights reserved
CLAUDIA SMART

ISBN # 978-1-79477-136-9

Library of Congress # 1-8160052237
CSMARTBOOKS

To All my beautiful neighbors! With love,

Claudia

Contents

Preface 4
Dedication 14
Acknowledgments 15
Introduction 17
Chapter One 27
    What GREAT NEWS IS THIS! 43
    Forgiveness 49
    Faith without Works Is Dead / Exercising Forgiveness 54
Chapter Two 64
    Body, Soul, and Spirit 64
    The Body 70
    The Soul 71
    The Spirit 72
    Faith and Endurance 73
Chapter Three 80
    Religion & Spirituality 80
Chapter Four 88
    Can We Control Our Thoughts? 88
Chapter Five 96
    Worshipping Our Thoughts or Our King? ... 96

Chapter Six..105
   Why on Earth Do Bad Things Happen?......................105
   "Why do bad things happen?" 105
Chapter Seven...111
   My Story..111
   Marriage...119
Chapter Eight..137
   Codependence & How to Heal From It......................137
Epilogue..159
References..167

Preface

"The grass withers and the flowers fall, but the word of our God endures forever"

(Isaiah 40:8 NIV)

Inspired by a true story, the author's real-life testimony and personal relationship with God through JESUS CHRIST has been an encouragement for many. God equips everyone in His Word with everything they need. Within these pages you will find tools the Lord provides to help you understand more about your existence and take to heart the LOVE your FATHER in heaven has for you! You will also find wisdom and understanding, virtue, knowledge, self-control, perseverance, godliness, kindness, and love to help you live boldly and confidently with more of the identity of Christ you were purposely called to have. It is necessary that we believe that we are very important to Him. He wrote His Word to us so we can know Him better and we can take each word to heart. Under the Umbrella of the Almighty will encourage you to choose to believe His Word is TRUTH and His LOVE for you is REAL!

You will know that you are surely Under the Umbrella of The Almighty even when you don't understand Him, feel Him or see Him. The Prophet

Isaiah understood this very well and explained it like this in GODS Word:

(Isaiah 55:8-9 NIV)

"For my thoughts are not your thoughts, neither are your ways my ways, declares the Lord. As the heavens are higher than the earth, so are my ways higher than your ways and my thoughts than your thoughts"

Also, King David reassured to us about His faithfulness and His protection on this beautiful psalm;

Psalm 91:4 (NIV)

"He will cover you with his feathers, and under his wings you will find refuge; his faithfulness will be your shield and rampart."

At this very moment, what you believe about your own purpose and value affects every area of your life including how you think and feel, the way you react to circumstances, and how you approach God and your relationships around you. The author will explain together with God's Word how important it is to understand God's WILL in your life also to love Him and receive His love for you. When we do this, it will be easier to put Him first in everything we do and trust Him in every decision we make.

What is guiding your beliefs? Are they healthy and founded upon solid truth? Or are they constantly changing with the opinions of others, your own emotions or even what you see? Author personal stories and practical wisdom challenges you to go deeper and have a personal inventory about your life, let the one who knows you best be the One who guides your heart and mind the most. It's time for all of us to live in the amazing light of His acceptance, abundance, grace and strength. Learn to step out in love, faith and confidence in every area of your life! In these simple readings accompanied by Scripture, the author will inspire and encourage you to live a more liberated love and life-giving existence than you ever thought was possible. Your faith has not finished yet not until you're last breath and He is not finished with you YET, not until you understand His love for you! There is eternal hope in Christ! The grave is not the end for us! There is hope in the middle of all our circumstances!

The purpose of this book is to give you hope about HEAVEN, and not to make you fear or worry about the temporary problems, diseases, and failures of this life. If we seek Him every day to do His will, He will surely give us peace, wisdom, hope, faith, and the understanding we need daily. There is freedom in Christ! Let's dig in and discover the peace, love and purpose that you are looking for in your life.

Stop being pulled into the anxiety of disappointments by discovering how to better process unmet expectations and other painful situations. Here, you will recognize strategies of the enemy so you can stand firm and strong in His Word and persevere through unsettling relationships and uncertain outcomes. God is protecting and preparing us even when we do not see it. In the end, our freedom and healing is what we are looking for in every area of our lives so that we can encourage others and help them navigate hard realities with the real help from God's truth. Freedom in our minds Freedom in our emotions, Freedom in our hearts and Freedom in our souls! This is what really is going to bring a Godly purpose in our lives. We can only change ourselves no one else but US! We can also learn how to be an encouragement to others even in our darkest seasons and in the middle of our circumstances.

Unfortunately, we've all had friends, family members and loved ones who said negative, discouraging words to us about discovering our faith, not because they don't love us or Him, but because of their lack of knowledge in Him. Sometimes this happens when we are about to make the best and most important decisions in our lives concerning our FAITH, our relationship with God and our own SALVATION! We need to understand we have to follow our own path, the one that will change us! We have to discover what is going to transformed us personally, yes it is ok to share, respect or follow some of our parent's tradition and faith, but our personal faith is only between You and God no one else. In the end, when we take our last breath it will be between God and us. Scripture is clear about this in; (Mark 10:28-30)

"Then Peter spoke up, 'We have left everything to follow you!' 'Truly I tell you,' Jesus replied, 'no one who has left home or brothers or sisters or mother or father or children or fields for me and the gospel will fail to receive a hundred times as much in this present age: homes, brothers, sisters, mothers, children and fields—along with persecutions—and in the age to come eternal life."

See we were made to enjoy reading His Word, to believe and worship Him! This book called the Bible, Gods Word is the best love letter we have all received and is hand-printed by Him! Yes! You're Daddy in Heaven! The Bible is our life manual and is in here, where we can truly know God and everything about our existence.

It is in His Word, where our thoughts and actions are tested, trained to live in this temporary life for Him.

Many around us have made promises they

were not able to keep. For many of us, our lives have been forever changed in those moments, and with each disappointment, we begin to feel like no one keeps their promises these days. But that's not true. While others may make promises and do break them, GOD never does.

Whatsoever He promises, He fulfills them in His timing and according to His will. The author believes the best promise of all is our ETERNAL LIFE with Him! And her passion is to get you excited and give you HOPE about the reality of heaven. Also, she wants to plant a seed of faith in your heart mind and spirit about His presence in your life at all times!

In this book, you will take to heart the promises of God about His love for you. You will read and believe in them, and instead of reading His words with your mind with your reasoning, you will receive them and believe them in your heart. God is with you; he will guide you, help you, and sustain you.

The author has come to an understanding that we should never forget that God is Holy and because He is, it is not hard for Him to keep all His promises! He is the ultimate Promise Keeper. God's promises are unfailing, unchanging, and true. Under the Umbrella of the Almighty's mission is to help you love God greatly with your lives. The journey you will take on this book will take you to a great place of understanding about Him, his unconditional, perfect love that will never end.

We have to know and learn what he says about us if we say we know Him. His Words are where we can get His identity, His comfort and guidance! Why not believe in the words of our best and greatest encourager? There is nothing more beautiful than to start reading a book full of hope and tools to fight our rejections, our insecurities OUR FEARS, and our faithless behaviors! We do not have to know it all, but we do have to understand His Word because it is the best manual for our lives. So, to start the author wants to deliver you personally the best love letter you have ever received in a long time and is called; The Father's love letter to you! He is in complete control of your life. His words are the only place we can find confirmation, comfort, hope, and healing. His Word is everlasting and services as our source of truth! Now received these words because they are handwritten by God for you!

"My Child, You may not know me, but I know everything about you. I know when you sit down and when you rise up. I am familiar with all your ways. (Psalm 139:1) "Even the very hairs on your head are numbered." (Matthew 10:29-30) "For you were made in my image."

"In me you live, and move and have your being. For you are my offspring." (Acts17:28) *"I knew you even before you were conceived." (Jeremiah 1:4-5)* *I chose you when I planned creation. (Ephesians 1:11) You were not a mistake, for all your days are written in my book. (Psalm 139:15-16)*

I determined the exact time of your birth and where you would live. (Acts 17:26) You are fearfully and wonderfully made. (Psalm 139:14) I knit you together in your mother's womb, (Psalm 139:13) and brought you forth on the day you were born. (Psalm 71:6) I have been misrepresented by those who do not know me. (John 8:41-44).

I am not distant and angry but am the complete expression of love, (1 John 4:16) and it is my desire to lavish my love on you. (1 John 3:1) Simply because you are my child and I am your Father. (1 John3:1)

I offer you more than your earthly father ever could. (Matthew 7:11) For I am the perfect father. (Matthew 5:48) Every good gift that you receive comes from my hand. (James 1:17) For I am your provider and I meet all your needs. (Matthew 6:31-33) My plan for your future has always been filled with hope. (Jeremiah 29:11) Because I love you with an everlasting love. (Jeremiah 31:3)

My thoughts toward you are countless as the sand on the seashore. (Psalm 139:17-18) And I rejoice over you with singing. (Zephaniah 3:17) I will never stop doing good to you. (Jeremiah 32:40) For you are my treasured possession. (Exodus 19:5)

I desire to establish you with all my heart and all my soul. (Jeremiah 32:41) And I want to show you great and marvelous things. (Jeremiah 33:3) If you seek me with all your heart, you will find me. (Deuteronomy 4:29) Delight in me and I will give you the desires of your heart. (Psalm 37:4) For it is I who gave you those desires. (Philippians 2:13)

I am able to do more for you than you could possibly imagine. (Ephesians 3:20) For I am your greatest encourager. (2 Thessalonians 2:16-17) I am also the Father who comforts you in all your troubles. (2 Corinthians 1:3-4)

When you are brokenhearted, I am close to you. (Psalm 34:18) As a shepherd carries a lamb, I have carried you close to my heart. (Isaiah 40:11) One day I will wipe away every tear from your eyes. (Revelation 21:34) And I'll take away all the pain you have suffered on this earth. (Revelation 21:3-4)

I am your Father, and I love you even as I love my son, Jesus. (John 17:23) For in Jesus, my love for you is revealed. (John 17:26)

He is the exact representation of my being. (Hebrews 1:3) He came to demonstrate that I am for you, not against you. (Romans 8:31) And to tell you that I am not counting your sins. (2 Corinthians 5:18-19) Jesus died so that you and I could be reconciled. (2 Corinthians 5:18-19) His death was the ultimate expression of my love for you. (1 John 4:10) I gave up everything I loved that I might gain your love. (Romans 8:31-32) If you receive the gift of my son Jesus, you receive me. (1 John 2:23) And nothing will ever separate you from my love again. (Romans 8:38-39)

Come home and I'll throw the biggest party heaven has ever seen. (Luke 15:7) I have always been Father, and will always be Father. (Ephesians 3:14-15)

My question is…Will you be my child? (John 1:12-13)

I am waiting for you. (Luke 15:11-32)

Love, Your Dad Almighty God.

Dedication

I owe my life to You, Jesus, because of what you did for me on the cross. You opened up my eyes of understanding; you forgave all my sins; my past, my present, and my future ones! You rescued me from my emotions and troubles and gave me Your Spirit to guide me in this life! I found my life manual in Your Eternal Word! This book is dedicated to You! Having the relationship I have with You today, the family You have given me, the Peace that surpasses all understanding, the Joy, the Hope, and identity I have in YOU, makes me want to share this book around the world to show what you have done! I am grateful, for you to have put this gratitude deep in my heart and I have come to realize that everything good comes from my perfect Father in heaven. I also dedicate this book to my friends and family who loved me just the way I am. God, may Your Spirit fill their hearts and minds with your love and knowledge with which you inspired me in writing this book. Seeing people get free in Christ and having more of Your love and Your Word in their hearts is my passion. Without hearing their stories or sharing my story, there is no testimony of how real you are to me! You are surely moving, not just in my life daily but with many around the world!

Acknowledgments

I want to acknowledge my cousin, who introduced me to the Lord in the year 2005 and also encouraged me to write 15 years ago. She saw this beautiful gift that God gave me of expressing myself, and she knew it would touch many with His love.

Also, so grateful to my husband, who encourages me every day to continue having my faith firmly in Christ. Thankful for his love and obedience to Christ in seeking His will in our lives and being the best Daddy for our son Isaiah.

Special thanks also to Celebrate Recovery that has allowed me to share some of my testimonies in their groups, and surely this book will be delivered to them with much love.

Also, special thanks to my friend, sister in Christ, and mentor Kimberly Stevens from Alberta Canada! Who I love so much for being there for me, listening to me, encouraging me, loving me, and praying for me.

And finally, and most importantly, The Holy Spirit, who inspired me with a passion for sharing my life and wisdom He has poured out in me all these years. Your hope and Your Word is an anchor for my soul and the best manual for my life!

I have undoubtedly received and surrender to Your Word and Your will and it is my honor to share what I have learned with all of your creation!

I want to thank you Lord for writing my life verse in your precious book! **(James 4:8 ESV), "Draw near to God, and he will draw near to you."**

Thank you, Jesus, for you have favored me with God and men! May your blessings be with me on this new journey as an Author. Protect this book with your precious blood and fill it with Your anointing. May Your presence be real and Your love revealed in Jesus name!

Introduction

We are so blessed to be part of this incredible walk of faith! All over the world, there is always something our loving, kind, omnipotent, omniscient and sovereign God is doing in so many hearts, souls, and minds. His Words are beautiful, true, alive, and it serves as a perfect life manual that we all need. We can confirm this in the book of Hebrews and believe in our hearts is real:

(Hebrews 4:12 ESV), "For the word of God is living and active, sharper than any two-edged sword, piercing to the division of soul and spirit, joints and marrow, and discerning the thoughts and intentions of the heart."

Yes, this is what God's words said. Isn't it powerful? He is changing so many lives, hearts, and minds right now with His Word. We are in a generation that needs so much of His healing, His truth, His Word foundation, and His support constantly. Inner healing and restoration are what we all need daily so that we can hear God and do His will.

The more healed and free we become, the

clearer the purpose our lives have! His word and His people are those who can help us through this healing process.

There are many awesome ministries, churches, and home bible study groups. It's amazing what the power of faith, hope, and love can do. I am so very grateful for all those ministries and people with such willing hearts that think of others more than themselves. They go the extra mile to help others, their marriages, and even their kids, with their walk with God. I am also grateful for all of those Christians who have also taken the steps of faith to share their testimonies and serve their God with passion. It's because of these testimonies that our faith increases, and we have come to know that we are second and He is first. Our faith grows when we hear and read His Words. The more we hear His Word, the stronger we get in our faith as described in **(Romans 10:17 KJV), "Faith comes by hearing and hearing by the Word of God."**

As the day draws closer to Christ's return, we see clearly the darkness and evilness of this world. We see a world, which hearts are filled with unforgiveness, pain, hurt, anger, hatred, and fear. A world that needs the peace of God and the real joy that only He can offer. This joy freely comes only from understanding His perfect grace and salvation from our sins in Jesus Christ. I have always realized that my everyday joy comes from knowing God loves me and I am on my way to heaven.

We must realize that the world and all the things in it are just temporary. John reminded us not to love this world or the things in this world. It's ok to enjoy them but not love them, but instead he said to guard this deep truth about our eternity in our souls.

"For everything in the world-the lust of the flesh, the lust of the eyes, and the pride of life comes not from the Father but from the world" (1 John 2:16 NIV).

For example, our money, home, beauty, work, and even our own life's bodies are temporary. They are fragile and like a vapor; Gods word describes it like this in **(James 4:14 NLV), "How do you know what your life will be like tomorrow? Your life is like the morning fog—it's here a little while, then it's gone: like a vapor."** In **(Psalm 39:4)**, the psalmist is saying; **"LORD, make me to know my end, and the measure of my days, what it is; that I may know how frail I am"**

Job also understood this very well. He had everything a man could want in life. He had riches, a beautiful family, a great reputation, and many more blessings that God gave him here on this earth. One day, it was all taken away. It's not that God wanted to punish Job, but rather He wanted to test him. He knew that it was only when Job could realize the source of his blessings rather than the blessing themselves, that Job would gain an eternal perspective; the exact perspective God wanted him to have. I have news for you reading this now; The Lord wants the very same perspective for you too. The book of Job was written so that we can learn and grow from his past experiences, tests, and mistakes that he went through. When we learn from other's mistakes, the bible calls that wisdom. Here's what Job said below just when he was going through one of the toughest trials of his life.

"Naked I came from my mother's womb, and naked I will depart: The Lord gave, and the Lord has taken away; may the name of the Lord be praised" (Job 1:21 NIV).

All these things above that we previously discussed have one thing in common; they are mortal. This means that one day we will be without them, and I have news for you. You cannot take them to heaven! Everything we have is His! We can be wise by leaving it to our kids, and teach them to take care of them but one day, they will also know everything they received is temporary. Paul did talk about the very three things here on earth that will eternally be with us forever. Those are faith, hope, and love.

"And now these three remain: faith, hope, and love. But the greatest of these is love" (1 Corinthians 13:13 NIV).

The Lord wants us to invest our time, money, and efforts in these three things. Why? Well, you guessed it, because they are eternal. For example, only His love can truly fill the voids in our hearts. Only faith can get us to heaven, where we can rest eternally with our magnificent Creator. As it is often said; without faith, it is impossible to please God. Only hope keeps us going each day that we don't get discouraged with depression and anxiety. Without it, we are hopeless.

There's a passage in Hebrews that further explains the importance of hope in our lives, and it highlights our lives without hope.

"Hope deferred makes the heart sick, but a longing fulfilled is a tree of life" (Proverbs 13:12 NIV).

So you can see the importance of eternal things that God is talking about. They actually have a direct effect on our souls. Jesus is often referred to in the New Testament as the "anchor of our souls," think about that for a minute. Have you ever been out on a boat? If you are in the ocean and turn off the engine of the boat, you don't just automatically stay in one spot. So, if you want to go for a swim, how do you keep your boat in one place? With waves and currents from all your sides pulling you everywhere, there's only one solution, an anchor. It helps keep you in one spot, so you either don't drift further out to the sea or so that your boat doesn't end up on shore in an accident. Well, Jesus is that anchor for our souls. He helps to keep us spiritually, mentally, and emotionally stable. Instead of alcohol or drugs, bad relationships, food, overspending, or other addictions, He wants to fill those voids in our hearts and lives. Only then can we be able to live the life that God wants us to live here on earth? Look what Jesus said here:

"The thief comes only to steal and kill and destroy; I have come that they may have life, and have it to the full" (John 10:10 NIV).

A lot of you reading this may think, God is so strict and has so many rules. If I follow them, I can't possibly enjoy my life. That couldn't be further from the truth. See, the scripture says that Satan comes to steal, kill, and destroy and that Jesus comes to bring life to the fullest. In other words, He wants you to live a complete life possible. As your Creator, the one who designed you with His original blueprint, He knows what will truly help you, and also what will harm you. He doesn't give us rules to be sad or to be mean, but rather to protect us from the harm that certain decisions will cause to our lives. This brings me to my next point. Who do you really believe God is? Is He truly all-loving?

"Greater love has no one than this: to lay down one's life for one's friends" (John10:10).

See, the way you see God will determine if you listen to Him or not. We all had imperfect families, whether it is the father or mother who tried their very best to raise us. In some cases, you may have experienced an abusive father, mother, or other family members you were raised with. They also tried the very best they could, and maybe in a lot of ways, they failed. God never failed. When Jesus came to do the will of the Father here on earth, He took on flesh.

That means He was fully God, and fully flesh at the very same time. He had a will like ours, the very ability to make choices, the very ability to sin. Yet, the bible says He was without sin. He died a sinner's death and yet didn't sin himself. He did this to demonstrate His perfect love in our lives.

"For we do not have a high priest who is unable to sympathize with our weaknesses, but one who in every respect has been tempted as we are, yet without sin" (Hebrews 4:15 NIV).

"So we fix our eyes not on what is seen, but

on what is unseen since what is seen is temporary, but what is unseen is eternal." (2 Corinthians 4:18 NIV).

God's mercy knows no boundaries for us. We need to believe that He has created Heaven for us, and this is not it! He is aware of our existence and always watching over us; He is in complete control. God's word said it like this: **"The heavens declare the glory of God, and the firmament shows His handiwork" (Psalm 19:1 NIV).** Everything that God has made, be it you and me, or wildlife, or angels, or stars and planets, has been created for His glory. When we see a breathtaking view of the Milky Way or peer at Saturn through a telescope, we are amazed at the wonders of God!

David wrote, **"I consider your heavens, the work of your fingers, the moon and the stars, which you have ordained" (Psalm 8:3 NIV).** When we see the vast number of stars, then read that scientists have discovered thousands upon thousands of galaxies, each containing millions of stars, we should be standing in reverent fear of God; so immense to make all that and call it the work of His fingers! Furthermore, (Psalm 147:4 NIV) tells us that **"He counts the number of the stars; He calls them all by name"** It is impossible for mankind to know how many stars there are, not to mention the "name" of every star! **"Indeed My hand has laid the foundation of the earth, and my right hand has stretched out the heavens; when I call to them, they stand up together" (Isaiah 48:13 NIV).**

Space and planets were created for God's glory. We know that stars and planets outside earth exist, and these, too, were created for the glory of God. The next star farther than the sun is over four light-years away, and that isn't even a measurable fraction of the size of the known universe, expanding or not. God is still the Creator and Controller of all things, and all things were made for His glory; including You! I mean for me to read this and then know the earth rotates once every 23 hours, 56 minutes and 4.09053 seconds, called the sidereal period, and its circumference is roughly 40,075 kilometers and not believe it is foolish! Also, to know the surface of the earth at the equator moves at a speed of 460 meters per second--or roughly 1,000 miles per hour! It is crazy for me not to believe there is a magical supernatural and powerful God that loves us very much! God said 310 times in His Word that he loves us! So, to think a minute without believing that an omniscient mind planned and designed our amazing planet is just again so foolish!

"In His hand are the deep places of the earth; the strength of the hills is His also. The sea is His, and He made it, and His hands formed the

dry land. Oh, come, let us worship and bow down; let us kneel before the Lord our maker" (Psalm95:4-6). (https://www.icr.org/article/planet-earthplan-or-accident).

We need to believe this Walk of Faith to obtain freedom so we can obtain all His blessings, meaning real blessings like peace, faith, purpose, joy, and supernatural love even when we don't feel it. When we invite His presence, all of His promises will truly come to our lives. Knowing God will help us realize He is the one giving us all those blessings.

See, when we don't know Him, we think it is luck or coincidence, but when He is present, we acknowledge Him and this brings peace. Obedience in wanting to read and obey His Word is better than the sacrifices we make, as we do this all His promises in His timing will come through and in faith and patience you will see them fulfill each one in your life.

Chapter One

I am so in awe of how this walk of faith has brought sanctification and purpose to me and a great number of people all over the world. I can see it so clearly that when we surrender to His will and His call, He is the only one who can change us. When we love others, the "Terms and Conditions" always apply. But God's love for us is above and beyond any conditions. He loves us unconditionally, and there is nothing that can separate us from His love. You are important to God and His word is the only truth that can set you free and on your way for sanctification! What is this word? Well, this is how the dictionary describes it: Sanctification is that renewal of our fallen nature by the Holy Spirit received through faith in Jesus Christ, whose blood of atonement cleanseth from all sin; whereby we are not only delivered from the guilt of sin, but are washed from its pollution, saved from its power, and are enabled, through grace, to love God. Sanctification is God's will for us **(1 Thessalonians 4:3).** The word sanctification is related to the word saint; both words have to do with holiness. To "sanctify" something is to set it apart for special use; to "sanctify" a person is to make him holy. "Sanctify them by the truth; His Word is the truth." Sanctification is a state of separation unto God; all believers enter into this state when they are born of God: **"You are in Christ Jesus, who became to us wisdom from God, righteousness, and sanctification, and redemption" (1 Corinthians 1:30 ESV).**

The sanctification mentioned in this verse is a once-for-ever separation of believers unto God. It is a work God performs, an intricate part of our salvation and our connection with Christ. See, whoever believes and puts their trust in Jesus, is a saint! Many get confused about this and think or believe you have to do rituals and be devoted to God to be a saint. No! You don't, God is clear. The only thing that makes you a saint, holy and pure is Jesus righteousness in you! Is your heart filled with His presence love faith and Eternal Word! We are not the miracle makers, only God! When we pray for others, we do it in faith and obedience but He is the one who decides when and how to perform that miracle! We just have to trust Him! He has gifted us with faith and His Word and by obedience, we do His will on this earth.

While we are positionally holy ("set free from every sin" by the blood of Christ, **(Acts 13:39)**, we know that WE STILL SIN. Sanctification is the effect of obedience to the Word of God in one's life. It is the same as growing in the Lord **(2 Peter 3:18)** or spiritual maturity. God started the work of making us like Christ, and He is continuing it until our strength fails, and the end draws near and our time has come **(Philippians 1:6).** We always need to pursue sanctification.

Little by little, every day, "those who are being sanctified" **(Hebrews 10:14 ESV)** are becoming more like Christ. Sanctification and a genuine relationship with God are what we need to seek; this will surely fill you with his understanding and eternal wisdom.

We are happier when we are living in His perfect Will, and this should be our prayer every day! His Word will change the way you see God and you will surely understand you have always been under the Umbrella of the Almighty all along!

There is an American band called "I Am They" that composes Christian music. They performed a song I loved titled "Scars" written by Ethan Hulse, Jon Mcconnell, Matthew Armstrong, and Matthew Hein. This song describes my feelings and my beliefs perfectly on why I started this relationship with Him. This is because my scars brought me to know more about Him. The song goes like this:

> *"Waking up to a new sunrise*
> *Looking back from the other side*
> *I can see now with open eyes*
> *Darkest water and deepest pain*

*I wouldn't trade it for anything
Cause my brokenness brought me to you
And these wounds are a story you'll use*

*So I'm thankful for the scars
'Cause without them I wouldn't know your heart And I know they'll always tell of who You are So forever I am thankful for the scars*

*Now I'm standing in confidence
With the strength of your faithfulness
And I'm not who I was before
No, I don't have to fear anymore*

*I can see, I can see
How you delivered me
In Your hands, In Your feet
I found my victory"*

When I started writing this book, I had many questions that I wrote in my journal, questions that little by little, one day at a time, I found the answers.

This brought peace to my soul and comfort to my mind about my existence.

Who am I?
What am I here for in this world?
Do I know how long I am to be here?

What is my purpose here?
Who should I trust?
Where should I go for guidance?
Should I worry about tomorrow?
What is really important in life?
Should I say why God doesn't answer my prayers or show up and fix my problems right away?
What should I be doing while I am waiting for God's answers?
What should I do when bad thoughts or uncomfortable thoughts come into my mind?
How can I handle temptation?
How can I control anger when people hurt me?
Why is it that we see too many wars and killings in our world?
Why do we see too much anger, sadness, and sickness?
Why do we always say, "If God exists, why is He letting these horrible things happen on this earth?
Why do we die?
Where do we go when we die?
Do angels exist?
Should we judge others?
Who is the only one that can judge?
Is judging a sin?
Is love the solution?
Who is the devil or Satan?
Is prayer a solution to all our problems?
What does a spiritual battle mean?

There are many questions at the same time, right? Questions that always echo in our minds and hearts. This is how I figure it out. It's a bit tough, but if you persevere and focus on what you truly want to believe, believe me, you will get the answers that will bring peace to your soul. It is a matter of being obedient with all your heart, believing in who you are, and seeking His Word all the time. Not just reading His Word but being diligent on hearing His Word in Christian Television, on radio stations, and wherever His presence takes you! But to do this, you need to receive Jesus and love God with all your heart, all your soul, and your entire mind first. Wanting to seek Him is the key and the power to know Him!

How do we know His Word is True? I found this truthful article and I wanted to share it with you:

How do we know the Bible is true?

"The combination of internal consistency, connection to evidence, and relevance to our experience makes the Bible unique among books. Like many religious works, the Bible claims to be true (2 Timothy 3:16). Unlike any other religious work, the Bible emphatically supports that assertion. The Bible not only encourages readers to examine their own beliefs (1 John 4:1), but it also commends those who check spiritual claims for truth (Acts 17:11). The Bible makes claims on the basis of history and eyewitnesses (Luke 1:1–4; 2 Peter 1:16), connects belief to visible evidence (John 20:30–31), and ties biblical ideas to the observable world (Psalm 19:1; Romans 1). Jesus overtly claimed to represent an exclusive truth (John 18:37; 14:6). So the Bible is clearly meant to be interpreted as true, and exclusively **true** (John 17:17). The Bible makes claims about the creation of the universe, the nature of the God who created the universe and reigns supremely over it, and the fate of mankind. If these claims are true, then the Bible is the most important book in the history of mankind.

If the Bible is true, then it holds the answers to life's biggest questions: "From where did I come?" "Why am I here?" and "What happens to me when I die?" The importance of the Bible's message demands it receives fair consideration, and the truthfulness of its message is observable, testable, and able to withstand scrutiny. The Bible should not be confused with a science textbook, but that does not mean that the Bible does not speak to issues that are scientific in nature. The water cycle was described in Scripture centuries before it was a scientific discovery. In some cases, science and the Bible have seemed to be at odds with each other. Yet, when science has advanced, the scientific theories have proved wrong and the Bible proved right. For example, it used to be standard medical practice to bleed patients as a cure for illness. Many people died because of excessive blood loss. Now medical professionals know that bloodletting as a cure for most diseases is counterproductive. The Bible always taught that "the life of a creature is in the blood" (Leviticus 17:11). The Bible's truth claims concerning world history have also been substantiated. Skeptics used to criticize the Bible for its mention of the Hittite people (e.g., 2 Kings 7:6). The lack of any archaeological evidence to support the existence of a Hittite culture was often cited as a rebuttal against Scripture. In 1876, however, archaeologists discovered evidence of the Hittite nation, and by the early 20th century, the vastness of the Hittite nation and its influence in the ancient world was common knowledge. The scientific and historical accuracy of the Bible is important evidence of the Bible's trustworthiness, but the Bible also contains fulfilled prophecies. Some of the biblical writers made claims about future events centuries in advance. If anyone of the events predicted had occurred, it would be astounding. But the Bible contains many, many prophecies. Some of the predictions were fulfilled in a short amount of time

(Abraham and Sarah had a son, Peter denied Jesus three times, Paul was a witness for Jesus in Rome, etc.). Other predictions were fulfilled hundreds of years later. The 300 messianic prophecies fulfilled by Jesus could not have reasonably been fulfilled by one person unless some greater power was involved. Specific prophecies like Jesus' birthplace, activities, manner of death, and resurrection demonstrate the preternatural accuracy of Scripture. When it is put to the test, the Bible is proved true in every area. Its truth extends to the spiritual, as well. That means that when the Bible says the Hittite nation existed, then we can believe that there were Hittites, and when the Bible teaches that "all have sinned" (Romans 3:23) and the "wages of sin is death" (Romans 6:23), then we need to believe that, too, because our conscience confirms this. Our conscience is our inner feeling or voice viewed as acting as a guide to the rightness or wrongness of one's behavior. When the Bible tells us that "God demonstrates his love for us in this: While we were still sinners, Christ died for us" (Romans5:8) and that "whoever believes in [Jesus] shall not perish but have eternal life" (John 3:16), then we can and should believe that, also. Understanding the Bible is important because the Bible is God's Word. When we open the Bible, we read God's message to us. What could be more important than understanding what the Creator of the universe has to say? We seek understanding of the

Bible for the same reason a man seeks to understand a love letter from his sweetheart. God loves us and desires to restore our relationship with Him **(Matthew 23:37)**. God communicates His love to us in the Bible **(John 3:16;1 John3:1;4:10)**. Copyright 2002- 2019 Got Questions Ministries."

Why is reading His Word with our hearts so important?

Because when you read or hear His word with only your mind, these questions will never become true and real in your life; instead, they will vanish. I have asked many times to several people, have you read the bible? The first thing they answered is yes, like seven times! I asked, do you understand it? They said no, it's just history. This means it was just their reasoning at work, not their hearts. If you read God's word with your heart and your mind together, you will understand and receive the real answers you are looking for and then freedom will come! We have to make our decision to love God and give Him a chance to love us in our lives. Here, I am not talking about loving God in "I love God" way and you do not even get to know Him but just acknowledge Him. I mean "loving God" is about having a personal relationship with Him daily. You need to have a relationship in which you can talk, understand, trust, and get to know Him to receive His love, His peace, and His answers.

See when we read the book of proverbs, we obtain wisdom, instruction, knowledge, and understanding and it all begins with fearing God. When we read the Psalms, we learn how to worship God and praise Him, something we need to do not just once a week but every day because it is medicine for our bodies and souls. By reading God's Word, we can discover is the best and most important book to read, with 66 books that will transform your life daily.

Again it is impossible to fill out the emptiness, the void we all have inside of us without inviting Jesus in our hearts and in our minds. It is also impossible to love someone else genuinely before we love God and we learn to love ourselves. To truly love ourselves, we need to discover who we are through Jesus Christ. Our insecure, negative thoughts will never let us grow of what we want to be if we are not close to the most wonderful Father and Savior of all.

How can that be so difficult?

How can our sins separate us from Him?

Well, we all have a free will and have the freedom to choose between many choices in life. The first one is we choose to live in this world and follow the customs that can't offer us more than what we see or feel, or we make the decision to start trusting and learning the things that really matter most in life and what was created since the beginning of time. To understand this and do it we need to start spending our time wisely. God's word explains this perfectly in the book of **(2 Corinthians 4:18 NIV,) So we fix our eyes not on what is seen, but on what is unseen, since what is seen is temporary, but what is unseen is eternal.**

From the very beginning of time, God had a purpose for His creation. In all His wisdom and greatness, He thought about us. It makes us feel special, right? See, one of the most powerful and important things God created along with us, is a Will. We have previously discussed this because it goes to the heart of Christianity, and the Gospel of Christ itself which I want to present in this book. A Will is a powerful thing. It is the freedom to choose and make decisions independently from anything or anyone. Nobody can take your will from you; only you can give your will away by the choices you make. The human will is so important it actually makes up 1/3 of our soul, as the soul consists of the mind, will, and emotions. Therefore, when God gave us free will, you had better believe it was important. As we look at the Word of God, you will see just how important it really is.

It goes back to the Garden of Eden, where God gave Adam a choice between eating the fruit of certain trees. Remember He told Adam he could eat from all the trees of the garden; just do not eat from the "Tree of Knowledge of Good and Evil." This was the very first evidence of free will in all of humanity. It was a choice where only Adam could choose himself, and nobody could choose for him. We all know Adam made the wrong decision and did eat from that exact tree God told him not to eat from. That was not a surprise to God, as the Lord knew Adam would make this wrong choice. Remember God is the Alpha and the Omega, the beginning and the end. Therefore, because the Lord saw the end and the beginning at the very same time, this was no surprise to Him. It is often hard for us humans to even begin to fully understand this because we are mortal. Jesus is immortal.

In the gospel of John, Jesus said, **"Truly, truly, I say to you, before Abraham was, I am." (John 8:58)**

This was Jesus stating to the Pharisees that He was, in fact, God. Not created, but rather the Creator. So the whole point here is that God not only doesn't make mistakes, but in His love, He has a plan for even our mistakes. By giving us a will, we have the ability to choose unlike a robot, which is programmed.

This is so vital to our lives, and God's ultimate plan in our lives. Imagine you tell your child they must give you a hug and a kiss everyday in the morning and the evening. If they were required to do so, when they did it, there wouldn't be much significance to it. Now, if your son or daughter freely came up to you when you got home from work and gave you a hug and a kiss it would mean so much more to you, right? Well, it's the same with God.

Our free will is powerful because it's an expression of who we are and our own very hearts towards God.

I also went through a few hardships in my life, but they did not break me, my soul, or my courage because I found the ultimate and eternal sources of strength in Jesus, His Word, and His people. These hardships brought meaning and purpose to my life. The purpose of sharing my story with you is to help you find Him personally and believe that His Word is our only and ultimate choice to find peace. Finding Him personally can also help us solve our problems, save ourselves from trouble in this world, and prepare our souls for our next life. Having God on our side brings comfort, identity and hope and this book is my testimony in this regard.

Every day, I have witnessed God doing amazing things through my bad days and good days. I realize that life is not easy! But I also realize that without God in your life and prayer, things could be worse.

Not everyone has the same challenge or the

same faith. We all live different lives in different circumstances, but we have one thing in common, we all have a void and emptiness in our hearts and minds that need to be filled with more understanding and love. Because we are all sinners in need of a savior, there is only one solution for everything, and it is the blood of our Savior, Jesus Christ. Without his blood, his forgiveness, his gift of eternal life, and his mercy, we couldn't have hoped to find Joy, Peace and Purpose in our lives to fill that void.

You indeed need to be persistent and open to believe. If you don't ask God for help, you make your part difficult for yourself to make it happen. It is not impossible for Him to come in difficult situations and help you if you don't even ask Him to do it. However, it is your choice to let Him in and make the first step to receiving Him in your life. Then His will in any circumstances will be done.

Again, God has given us free will in our lives. We can choose to follow the customs of this world, or we can choose to follow, believe, glorify, and Trust Him! This is exactly what God says in His Word, what are we going to choose?

His Word is very clear in the book of Romans:

(Romans 12 NLT) "And so, dear brothers and sisters, I plead with you to give your bodies to God because of all he has done for you. Let them

be a living and holy sacrifice—the kind he will find acceptable. This is truly the way to worship him. 2 Don't copy the behavior and customs of this world but let God transform you into a new person by changing the way you think. Then you will learn to know God's will for you, which is good and pleasing and perfect"

It is our absolute choice, and that is why it is so important to love God with all your heart. Stop trying to gain His love by performing religious rituals or unloving works and start obeying and following Him by reading His Word. A personal relationship is what He is looking for! At the end of our lives, it is just going to be between our Creator and us! No one else will be there, that is if you believe in eternal life. Again, that moment when you will have your last breath, it will be just you and God! God's love and purpose in your heart is what's going to bring you to do loving works or deeds.

"Trust in the Lord with all your heart, and do not lean on your understanding. In all your ways acknowledge him, and he will make straight your paths" (Proverbs 3:5-6 NLT).

When you start building a relationship with your redeemer, with your savior, you start seeing life differently. You will no longer go through life with a confused materialistic mind but with a spiritual one.

You will start preparing more for your eternal salvation than for this mortal world. Preparing for our eternal salvation means being more aware of our lives in receiving more of His sanctification to remove contamination that is separating us from God! Basically, it is just learning how to use your time wisely! You will start discovering what your purpose is, why God made you and chose you! Also, you will start finding out what your gifts are, and you will start thinking more about others than yourself.

We need to understand that our enemy (Satan) is always trying to get us, confusing us with our emotions and what we see, He blinds us, lies to us, and he does not want us to see the truth about our lives and our holy and pure existence. He just wants us to think that this mortal world and body is all we could ever get. He simply does not want any of us to go to heaven or enjoy this life with God. The more souls he has for his kingdom, the happier he will be! See, when Jesus said, "He has saved us," it means He rescued us from eternal condemnation, a place called Hell. Yes, this is real; our God is a just God.

What GREAT NEWS IS THIS!

I can tell you some good news, there is eternal life in Christ Jesus, and God loves you very much! He has a special plan for you! This life is not about all we have or see. He does not only wants you to go to heaven, but also wants you to live an abundant life in this world, that is full of His joy, full of His peace, full of His purpose, and full of His eternal love. He wants to use you to impart all this to others!

We need to start trusting and loving the One and Only God whom we are one day going to meet. We can choose to live our lives on our own strength and selfishness and never be able to see the vision that God wants us to see, or we can give Him glory and honor for all He does for us daily. I don't mean the vision of making it through life because we all make it, but I mean making it with the peace and understanding we deserve, enjoying every single moment of it, and understanding why we are here and what our calling and purpose is.

This is how we will start understanding why our lives sometimes get so difficult and we realized all of it is part of Gods plan!

God can help you by giving you His favor, His grace, His forgiveness, He could make anything possible for you, open doors for you, heal you, and give you the wisdom and strength you need. Isn't this good news? But you need to start choosing to seek

Him, be obedient, believe He loves you and be guided by the Holy Spirit. His Word is what we need to read every day to guide us and give us the strength grace and peace we need and this is to battle against the temptations, fears, insecurities, and the evil of this world daily.

The Holy Spirit is a gift from God that you have received because the Holy Spirit can help you in many ways. The Holy Spirit is good news to us because he can help us any time we invite him. He follows us everywhere we go, talks to us in our spirit, reveals things to us, corrects us, and protects us from making wrong choices. There are many misconceptions about the identity of the Holy Spirit. Some view the Holy Spirit as a mystical force; others understand the Holy Spirit as the impersonal power that God makes available to the followers of Christ.

What does the Bible say about the identity of the Holy Spirit? Simply put, the Bible declares that the Holy Spirit is God. The Bible also tells us that the Holy Spirit is a divine person, a being with mind, emotions, and will.

The fact that the Holy Spirit is God is clearly seen in many places in His Word. We can also understand that the Holy Spirit is God because He possesses the characteristics of Him, and if He is God in the third person of the Trinity, he will give us the power to walk in the ways of righteousness and give us the strength to make better choices. What great news again is this!

For example, His omnipresence is seen in:

(Psalm 139:7-8) "Where can I go from your Spirit? Where can I flee from your presence? If I go up to the heavens, you are there; if I make my bed in the depths, you are there"

Then in **(1 Corinthians 2:10-11 NIV)**, we see the characteristic of omniscience in the Holy Spirit:

"But God has revealed it to us by his Spirit. The Spirit searches all things, even the deep things of God. For who among men knows the thoughts of a man except the man's spirit within him? In the same way no one knows the thoughts of God except the Spirit of God."

We can know that the Holy Spirit is indeed a divine person because He possesses a mind, emotions, and will. The Holy Spirit thinks and knows **(1 Corinthians 2:10)**. The Holy Spirit can be grieved **(Ephesians 4:30)**. The Spirit intercedes for us **(Romans 8:26-27)**. He makes decisions according to His will **(1 Corinthians 12:7-11)**. The Holy Spirit is God, again, the Third Person of the Trinity. As God, the Holy Spirit can truly function as the Comforter and Counselor that Jesus promised He would be to us **(John 14:16, 26, 15:26)**.

In my spiritual journey, I learned that trusting in God and acknowledging the Holy Spirit is always the best option; it is safer than trusting what we can see. I can tell you that my life hasn't been easy, but I thank God for every little or big experience, bad and good, that has happened to me and will happen to me on this temporary life. This has matured me into the person I am now. See, our legacy and our future descendants will reap all that we sow in Him now! The closer I am to Him, the better choices my descendants and I will make. This is because His ways are higher than my ways.

Again, every one of us has a different life or are born in different lives, and that's why we all have different purposes in Him. This is just a process of experiences and a reason for our spiritual growth. Isn't this great news! What God sees is not your decisions and behaviors but your heart. When He sees turbulences and the anxiety that we all encounter in our lives, He gets sad, and He wants us to have faith for us to know that He is in control, and He wants us to be still and pray while he is fixing our situation or gives us the answer to help fix our situation! We can't believe or have the faith if we don't renew our minds because faith comes by hearing His word! With my life experiences, I can tell you why many things happened to me, even at a young age, and I see them today as a big, positive experience and growth. Today more than ever, I totally understand what God said in His word in the book of **(James 1: 2 NLT)**

"Dear brothers and sisters, when troubles of any kind come your way, consider it an opportunity for great joy. For you know that when your faith is tested, your endurance has a chance to grow. 4 So let it grow, for when your endurance is fully developed, you will be perfect and complete, needing nothing.

If you need wisdom, ask our generous God, and he will give it to you. He will not rebuke you for asking. But when you ask him, be sure that your faith is in God alone. Do not waver, for a person with divided loyalty is as unsettled as a wave of the sea that is blown and tossed by the wind. Such people should not expect to receive anything from the Lord. Their loyalty is divided between God and the world, and they are unstable in everything they do"

In fact, God has toughened me over time with troubles and pleasures. Because of this, I have become more loving and gracious with others! And I want this for you! See when we have good seasons in our lives, this means it is a time for preparation; it is a time to get stronger in our faith so that when a bad season comes, we are ready to overcome the season with peace, hope, strength and the wisdom and victory that we need. We need the peace that surpasses all understanding when we face trials and tribulations.

I was 29 years old at the time of starting writing this book. I gave my life and my heart to Him at 25, and today that I am 40 I haven't stopped sharing and writing about this joy and truth, and I do it because He has changed my life, and I AM, and I WILL always be thankful for that willingness to speak that He has put in my heart! What great news is for someone like me who was lost to be found!

Forgiveness

Finding Him, I came to an understanding about forgiveness.

"Be kind to one another, tenderhearted, forgiving each other, just as God in Christ has also forgiven you" (Ephesians 4:32. NLT).

Forgiveness is critical to our freedom due to the cross. God did not give us what we deserve; He gave us what we needed according to His mercy. We are to be merciful just as our heavenly Father is merciful **(Luke 6:36)**. We are to forgive as we have been forgiven **(Ephesians 4:31-32)**.

We will never understand we need forgiveness from God. Mostly, the influence that our enemy gets in the lives of Christians or non-Christians is because of unforgiveness. We are told to forgive others so that the enemy cannot take advantage of us **(2 Corinthians 2:10-11)**. God wants us to forgive others from our hearts **(Matthew 18:34-35)**.

Forgiveness does not mean forgetting. People who try to forget, find that they cannot. God says He will **"remember no more" our sins (Hebrews 10:17)**, but God, being omniscient, cannot forget. **"Remember no more"** means that God will never use the past against **us (Psalm 103:12)**.

Forgetting may be a result of forgiveness, but it is never the means of forgiveness. When we bring up the past and use it against others, we haven't forgiven them. Forgiveness is a choice, a crisis of the will, and issue of the heart. We choose to face and acknowledge the hurt and the hate to forgive from the heart.

Since God requires us to forgive, it is something we can do. He would never expect us to do something we cannot do. But forgiveness is difficult for us because it pulls against our concept of justice. We want revenge for offenses suffered. But we are told never to take our own revenge **(Romans 12:19)**. "Why should I let them off the hook?" we protest! You might let them off your hook, but they are never off God's hook. He will deal with them fairly, and it is something we cannot do. If you don't let offenses off your heart, you are going to be attached to the past, and it means constant pain for you.

We all seek freedom as it is the highest virtue. We want freedom because we consider that we are oppressed, and that is the worldly view of freedom. When we talk about freedom in Christ, it does not mean political or economic freedom. History tells us that some of the oppressed people had absolute freedom in Christ. The bible tells us that no one is free in a spiritual context. In Romans 6, the Apostle Paul says that we are slaves, either to sin or righteousness. Yes! We need to realize that self-righteousness is the enemy of forgiveness. When we think we are good with everyone, that's when we fall short! Every day we struggle with unforgiveness and offenses with ourselves and with others, and that's why we need to make this choice of forgiving a permanent lifestyle because forgiveness is a decision, not an emotion. Growing closer to Him by praying every day for His love in us will help us fight this disease!

Those who are slaves to sin cannot free themselves from it. But once we are freed from the penalty and power of sin through the cross, we become a different kind of slave in which we find complete peace and true freedom.

It may seem a contradiction, but the true freedom in Christ comes to the ones who are His slaves. Generally speaking, slavery signifies degradation, hardship, and inequality. But the biblical standard is the true freedom of Christ's slaves who experience joy and peace as a result of true freedom in Christ in this life. In the New Testament, the word "Doulos" is mentioned 124 times; this means "someone who belongs to another" or "bond-slave with no possession rights of his own." However, the majority of modern bible versions including King James Version translate "Doulos" as "servant" or "bond-servant." The word "servant" means a person who is paid wages for his work and owes to something from their master. A Christian has nothing to offer the Lord in payment for his forgiveness, and he is fully owned by the Master who bought him with His shed blood on the cross. Christians have been bought by that blood and are eternally labeled with the ownership of God. We are not hired by God! We belong to Him.

"You, however, are not in the flesh but in the Spirit, if in fact, the Spirit of God dwells in

you. Anyone who does not have the Spirit of Christ does not belong to him" (Romans 8:9).

Thus, the appropriate translation of the word **"Doulos" is "Slave." When we are slaves of Christ, we become absolutely free from sins. "If the Son sets you free, you will be free indeed"** (John 8:36). Thus, the Christian can say along with Paul:

"For the law of the Spirit of life has set you free in Christ Jesus from the law of sin and death" (Romans 8:2).

"And you will know the truth, and the truth will set you free" (John 8:32).

With our bondage to Christ, we have become sons and heirs of the Highest God **(Galatians 4:1-7)**. As heirs, we get the inheritance of eternal life that God confers on all His children. This is a matchless honor that we could ever inherit in this world. The ones who choose to be in bondage to sin, inherit spiritual death and eternity in a place I don't like to mention too much but is real and is called hell.

The Bible has plenty to say about forgiveness and unforgiveness. The most well-known teaching on unforgiveness is Jesus' parable of the unmerciful servant in **(Matthew 18:21-35)**. In the parable, a king forgives an enormously large debt of one of his servants. Later, the same servant refuses to forgive a small debt of another man. When the king hears about it, he rescinds his prior forgiveness. Jesus concludes by saying,

"This is how my heavenly Father will treat each of you unless you forgive your brother or sister from your heart." (Matthew 18:35).

Do not be confused here! God's forgiveness is not based on our acts. Forgiveness and salvation are founded completely in the person of God and by Jesus' redeeming work on the cross. However, our actions demonstrate our faith and the extent to which we understand God's grace.

Faith without Works Is Dead / Exercising Forgiveness

"What good is it, my brothers, if someone says he has faith but does not have works? Can that faith save him? If a brother or sister is poorly clothed and lacking in daily food, and one of you says to them, "Go in peace, be warmed and filled," without giving them the things needed for the body, what good is that? So also faith by itself, if it does not have works, is dead. But someone will say, "You have faith, and I have works." Show me your faith apart from your works, and I will show you my faith by my works. 19 You believe that God is

one; you do well. Even the demons believe—and shudder! Do you want to be shown, you foolish person, that faith apart from works is useless? Was not Abraham our father justified by works when he offered up his son Isaac on the altar? You see that faith was active along with his works, and faith was completed by his works; and the Scripture was fulfilled that says, "Abraham believed God, and it was counted to him as righteousness"—and he was called a friend of God. You see that a person is justified by works and not by faith alone. And in the same way, was not also Rahab the prostitute justified by works when she received the messengers and sent them out by another way? For as the body apart from the spirit is dead, so also faith apart from works is dead" (James 2:14-26).

"Therefore I tell you, her sins, which are many, are forgiven—for she loved much. But he who is forgiven little loves little" (Luke 7:47).

We are completely unworthy, yet Jesus chose to pay the price for our sins and to give us forgiveness **(Romans 5:8)**. When we truly grasp the greatness of God's gift to us, we will extend the gift to others. We have been given grace and should give grace to others in return. In the parable, we are appalled at the servant who would not forgive a minor debt after having been forgiven for his unpayable debt. When we are unforgiving unto others, we act just like the servant in the parable.

Unforgiveness also robs us of the full life God intends for us. Rather than promote justice, our unforgiveness festers into bitterness.

(Hebrews 12:14-15) warns: "Make every effort to live in peace with everyone and to be holy; without holiness; no one will see the Lord. See to it that no one falls short of the grace of God and that no bitter root rises up to cause trouble and defile many."

We also know that those who have sinned against us, whom we may not want to forgive are held accountable by God. Beloved, never avenge yourselves, but leave it to the wrath of God, for it is written, **"Vengeance is mine, I will repay, says the Lord" (Romans 12:19)**

"For we know him who said, "Vengeance is mine; I will repay." And again, "The Lord will judge his people." (Hebrews 10:30)

It is important to recognize that forgiving does not mean downplaying wrongdoing or reconcile. When we choose to forgive, we release a person from his indebtedness to us. We actually surrender the right to seek revenge, and we will not hold their wrongdoings against them. However, we do not necessarily allow that person back into our circle of trust or fully release them from the consequences of their wrongdoings. **(Romans 6:23)** tells us that **"the wages of sin is death"**

God's forgiveness does relieve us from eternal death, but it does not always release us from the death-like consequences of sin like a broken relationship or the penalty provided by the justice system. Forgiveness does not mean that we act as if no wrong had been done; it does mean we recognize that abundant grace has been given to us and that we have no right to hold others' wrongdoing over their heads.

Time and again, Gods Word calls us to forgive one another.

For instance, **(Ephesians 4:32)** says:

"Be kind and compassionate to one another, forgiving each other, just as in Christ, God forgave you."

We have been given much in the way of forgiveness, and much is expected from us in response.

"But the one who did not know, and did

what deserved a beating, will receive a light beating. Everyone to whom much was given, of him, much will be required, and from him to whom they entrusted much, they will demand the more" (Luke 12:48).

I know forgiveness is often a difficult task, but being unforgiving becomes disobedience to God and an attempt to depreciate the greatness of His gift.

Today, we can see that lots of Christians live as if they were still in bondage. In fact, we often show rebellious behavior against our Lord as we refuse to follow His word and stick to our old, sinful ways. It so happens because our new nature still lives in the old, fleshly nature, and we are drawn to follow sinful ways. The Apostle Paul tells the Ephesians to "Put Off" the old self with its deception and "Put On" the new self with its righteousness; put off lies and put on honesty, put off theft, and put on usefulness and work. Put off bitterness and rage, and put on sympathy and forgiveness **(Ephesians 4:22–32)**. We have been set free from the slavery of sin, but most of us choose to put the chains back on since part of us loves the old life.

We don't realize we have been crucified with Christ **(Galatians 2:20)**, and we have been born-again entirely as new creatures **(2 Corinthians 5:17)**. The Christian life is death to self and rising to "walk in the newness of life" **(Romans 6:4)**. This new life is characterized by true feelings about Him who saved us, not the thoughts of the dead flesh that has been crucified with Christ. When we keep thinking about ourselves and indulge in sins of flesh we have been freed from, we actually carry around a dead body that is full of rottenness and death. To bury it in entirety, we need the power of the Spirit, which is the only source of our strength, and we can do it by feeding our new nature on God's Word and through prayer. This way, we can obtain the strength we need to prevent the desire to get back to the old and sinful ways. Then only us can realize that our new status as slaves to Christ is true freedom, and we will call upon His strength to "let not sin reign in your mortal body so that you obey its evil desires" **(Romans 6:12)**.

Stop the pain; let it go. You don't forgive someone merely for his or her sake; you do it for your sake so you can be free. Your need to forgive isn't an issue between you and the offender; it's between you and God.

Trying to not take offense is like trying to not think about it. If someone says, "Don't think about it," we automatically think about them. If we focus on trying not to take offense, we will keep thinking about the offense. This principle applies to just about any sin a person can commit. When we focus on behavior, even in an attempt to eliminate it, the result is more of that behavior. This is just how our minds work.

Thankfully, there is another better way to address this problem.

"People are lured and enticed into sin as a result of their desire or wanting, which is the beginning of sinning" (James 1:14).

Every sin or bad behavior begins with desire. Desire itself is not bad because there are many good desires. But the desires that lead to sin are wrong desires because they are based on false perspectives and misplaced expectations about others and ourselves. To eliminate bad behavior, we must first discover the desire behind it.

Most people are inclined to taking offense at little things because of a false perspective of security. We all desire security and safety; we desire to have the good opinion of others. We can secure good opinions of others with performance, what we do, how we speak, how we dress, and how we express ourselves. When our security is based on our performance, we may feel vulnerable and threatened when others express negative things about us. The natural response is to take offense or get angry. Even a casual or a trivial remark can worry us and ruin our peace. To avoid taking offense, we need to address our desire for security and safety. The tendency to take offense will keep existing if our feelings of security are rooted in ourselves. If our feelings of security are not rooted in ourselves and with our performance, our viewpoint will change, and our response to others' remarks will not be balanced.

The book of Proverbs tells us twice to "cover" offenses in **(Proverbs 10:12, 17:9)**. The covering of offense is related to love. **(1Peter 4:8)** says, **"Love covers over a multitude of sins"**, and that "multitude" would have to include small slights. In any relationship, there are numerous exasperating things that should just be "covered" for the sake of love. By covering offenses, we actually empathize with the offender and extend the benefit of the doubt. Maybe, the offenders did not mean what they said; maybe, we misheard; maybe, the offender was having a bad day or wasn't thinking straight at that time. When we cover the offense of others, it helps us too. Forgiveness is honorable and the reminder that your security is not based on others' opinions of you but on the security that you have in Christ.

"A person's wisdom yields patience; it is to one's glory to overlook an offense" (Proverbs 19:11).

"He predestined us for adoption to himself as sons through Jesus Christ, according to the purpose of his will, 6 to the praise of his glorious grace, with which he has blessed us in the Beloved.

In him, we have redemption through his blood, the forgiveness of our trespasses, according to the riches of his grace" *(Ephesians 1:5-7).*

Jesus told His disciples to pray for anything in His name, and they would obtain what they asked for. Do you believe that God wants you to be angry with others, or forgiving of them? Do you believe that your security is in Him rather than in yourself? If you pray and ask Him to help you not to take offense, He will surely answer your prayer. If you ask Him to remind you of His secure and steadfast love, He will answer your prayer. You can confidently pray for help in every offending situation.

"Let us then with confidence draw near to the throne of grace, that we may receive mercy and find grace to help in time of need" *(Hebrews 4:16).*

In Bethany, as Jesus was reclining on a table, a woman entered the room with an alabaster jar of a fine perfume. The woman broke the container and anointed Jesus' head with the fragrant ointment **(Mark 14:3)**. Immediately, she was criticized; in fact, "they rebuked her harshly" **(Mark 14:4-5)**. Taking offense would have been a natural response for her, but she didn't. While Jesus also defended her, "Leave her alone" **(Mark 14:6)**, the woman's love of Christ and her humble response to an offense were honored.

"Wherever the gospel is preached throughout the world and what she did is being told, it serves as a remembrance of her humble actions." (**Mark 14:9**).

To sum it up, when we take offense, it is because someone has hurt us or frightened us. God has given us two ways to deal with the offenses. First, by remembering that other persons also have things that hurt and frighten them. When we love the offender and focus on their needs, we will no longer notice their offenses. Secondly, by remembering that, when we belong to Christ, we are fundamentally secured in Him and do not need to react and defend ourselves, because He has promised to defend us (**Isaiah 35:3–4**). When we struggle to trust Him, all we need to do is pray for the strength, and we know that He will answer us (**John 14:13–14**).

With this prayer I would like to end this chapter: Lord, I stand amazed at the example of your forgiveness. I desire to grow in my willingness to forgive those who have hurt me in Jesus' Name.

Chapter Two

Body, Soul, and Spirit

Life can change at any moment; we live by faith every day. We wake up expecting that it is going to be a good day, but sometimes we don't see what we want to see, or we want to feel, and we think that God is not with us. But that's never true! Because God is always working in our lives. We just don't realize it, because we are impatient, or maybe we have very little faith. But when God changes your heart, which is the biggest miracle we can ever obtain from Him, we start to see life differently. That's why it is very important to be born again in spirit. See when we don't believe in Him, our spirit is dead but when we invite him, we are "born again." We become alive in Him!

"But if Christ is in you, then even though your body is subject to death because of sin, the Spirit gives life because of righteousness" (Romans 8:10 NIV).

Jesus said, "I am the resurrection and the life. The one who believes in me will live, even though they die; and whoever lives by believing in me will never die. Do you believe this?" (John

11:25-26 NIV)

The Bible confirms this again in **(Ephesians 2 NIV)** that we are made alive in Christ

"As for you, you were dead in your transgressions and sins, in which you used to live when you followed the ways of this world and of the ruler of the kingdom of the air, the spirit who is now at work in those who are disobedient. All of us also lived among them at one time, gratifying the cravings of our flesh and following its desires and thoughts. Like the rest, we were by nature deserving of wrath. But because of his great love for us, God, who is rich in mercy, made us alive with Christ even when we were dead in transgressions—it is by grace you have been saved. And God raised us up with Christ and seated us with him in the heavenly realms in Christ Jesus, in order that in the coming ages he might show the incomparable riches of his grace, expressed in his kindness to us in Christ Jesus. For it is by grace you have been saved, through faith—and this is not from yourselves, it is the gift of God— not by works, so that no one can boast."

What does "being born again" really mean?

Aren't we already born in this world?

Well, yes, we are already born, but we are born in our flesh. What I mean to say here refers to our spiritual rebirth. The purpose of God creating human beings was intended to establish a personal relationship with Him. He created us partly material and partly immaterial.

- The material part is tangible, which is a physical body, i.e., flesh, bones, and organs. The body, which is the material part, perishes with death.
- The immaterial part is intangible, which includes soul, spirit, intelligence, will, and conscience and they exist beyond the physical life cycle of a human being.

Mainly, the discussions revolve around us being a Tripartite or Bipartite. According to the bipartite viewpoint, we have the body and soul. Tripartite refers to the theory, which divides the human body into three parts; the body, soul, and spirit. In fact, the human body is highly complex, and it is only God who can have the power to create us as we are.

Thus, we all possess material and immaterial qualities. However, we need to understand what our

Lord says about our existence and the purpose. There are many verses in His Word that tell us about our purpose, such as **(Genesis 2:7),** which says that humans were created as living souls.

> **"Then the Lord God formed the man of dust from the ground and breathed into his nostrils the breath of life, and the man became a living creature" (Genesis 2:7).**

> "And they fell on their faces and said, O God, the God of the spirits of all flesh, shall one man sin, and will you be angry with all the congregation?" (Numbers 16:22).

> "Keep your heart with all vigilance, for from it flow the springs of life" (Proverbs 4:23).

(Numbers 16:22) is huge in meaning as it tells us that the spirits of God are possessed by all Mankind. Further, **(Proverbs 4:23)** tells us that the heart is key to humans' will and emotions and must be guided well.

And looking intently at the council, Paul said,

> "Brothers, I have lived my life before God in all good conscience up to this day" (Acts 23:1).

This is also a significant verse because it gives us the realization of our conscience that helps us differentiate between right and wrong. If a bad act does not shake our souls, it indeed indicates dead conscience.

"Do not be conformed to this world, but be transformed by the renewal of your mind, that by testing you may discern what is the will of God, what is good and acceptable and perfect" (Romans 12:2).

There are many verses that refer to the multiple facets of the immaterial part of human beings, and the Bible defines it far more than soul and spirit. There is a very good verse to understand it clearly.

"For the word of God is living and active, sharper than any two-edged sword, piercing to the division of soul and of spirit, of joints and of marrow, and discerning the thoughts and intentions of the heart." (Hebrews 4:12).

As we contemplate this verse, we can see two significant points in it:

- The soul and spirit can be divided.
- It is only our Lord who can make this division happen.

Here, the point I am driving from this is that we need to pay our absolute attention to our Lord, who has created us.

"I praise you, for I am fearfully and wonderfully made. Wonderful are your works; my soul knows it very well" (Psalm 139:14).

We know that we are partly material and partly immaterial, and together they make us a good human being. Thus, we do not need to separate them from one another to fully believe and follow our Lord.

"Now there was a man of the Pharisees named Nicodemus, a ruler of the Jews. This man came to Jesus by night and said to him, "Rabbi, we know that you are a teacher come from God, for no one can do these signs that you do unless God is with him." Jesus answered him, "Truly, truly, I say to you, unless one is born again he cannot see the kingdom of God." Nicodemus said to him, "How can a man be born when he is old? Can he enter a second time into his mother's womb and be born?" Jesus answered, "Truly, truly, I say to you, unless one is born of water and the Spirit, he cannot enter the kingdom of God. That which is born of the flesh is flesh, and that which is born of the Spirit is spirit. Do not marvel that I said to you, 'You must be born again." (John 3:1-7)

God has created human beings of three different parts, and **(1 Thessalonians 5:23)** shows it as **"Now may the God of peace himself sanctify you completely, and may your whole spirit and soul and body be kept blameless at the coming of our Lord Jesus Christ."**

The Body

The body is the pure manifestation of physical or material being. Our body is flesh created in the result of minerals and water. The body functions in harmony with the nature and spirit of our world. Our human body enables us to carry out our motor functions. Our nervous system enables us to connect to the world physically as we use five senses. The human body is born, develops, and matures. As time passes, the body starts declining and ultimately dies. Further, it decomposes and gets back into its basic elements, and onwards remains a particle in the dust of the world. This way, life on earth goes on! Our body is indeed a part of our being, but it is not everything that can define who WE really are. The human body has a limited life on the earth, but the soul lives forever.

"And at the end of your life you groan, when your flesh and body are consumed,.."

(Proverbs 5:11)

The Soul

The soul is our immaterial being, and it matters more than the physical body. It is our soul that shapes our beliefs. It is not an exaggeration to say that it is the soul that shows who WE truly are. The soul represents our individuality which was made in God's image; it represents our pure heart. Your soul was not in existence before you came into this world through your parents, but it will exist eternally then onward.

No matter how powerful a man is, he can never kill a soul, but our Lord only!

"And do not fear those who kill the body but cannot kill the soul. Rather fear him who can destroy both soul and body in hell" (Matthew 10:28).

The body and soul are together, and they may or may not live in harmony. They part with each other when the body dies as the soul abandons the body and enters the eternal life.

"And as her soul was departing (for she

was dying), she called his name Benoni; but his father called him Benjamin" *(Genesis 35:18)*.

The Spirit

Spirit is the fundamental source of power. It is your spirit that helps you control body and soul. It is the spirit that creates the difference between our good or bad existence. The spirit takes us into dark or shows us light; it is either of Satan or of God.

"But he turned and rebuked them, and said, you do not know what manner of spirit you are of" (Luke 9:55).

As the body dies, the soul departs to eternity. Now it depends on our personal relationship with God, whether we will be bestowed with rewards or bad things will welcome us. We need to realize that our soul is undying, and our gracious God gives us life and the absolute will to decide our destiny. There are very powerful verses to understand this fact and realize how gracious our God is.

"Jesus answered them, "Is it not written in your Law, 'I said, you are gods'?" *(John 10:34),*

"So, God created man in his own image, in the image of God he created him; male and female

he created them." *(Genesis 1:27)*.

"Tell us what is to come hereafter, that we may know that you are gods; do good, or do harm, that we may be dismayed and terrified"
(Isaiah 41:23).

"I said, "You are gods, sons of the Most High, all of you"*(Psalm 82:6)*.

Faith and Endurance

Have you ever heard someone that said the following: "How do we know the Bible is true", "Why should we believe something we can't prove is true?" To answer that question, I want to remind you that our belief in Christianity is a walk of faith. What is faith you may ask? Well according to **(Hebrews 11:1)**;

"Now faith is confidence in what we hope for and assurance about what we do not see."

Faith is the assurance in what we cannot see! You could also translate that into what we cannot readily prove. Meaning, we can't prove that God flooded the earth because we were not there. Nevertheless, it happened. We weren't there when Moses split the Red Sea, but it happened.

I want to encourage you to increase your **"faith" because faith comes by hearing and hearing by the Word of God" (Romans 10:17)**. So although we weren't there, when we read God's Word, it comes alive in our lives and our hearts as if we were there. Having this faith is what God wants. Why does God want us to have faith you may ask? I often wondered this very thing for many years of my life.

Why didn't God just reveal and prove everything all the time, or at least when people asked Him to do so? Well, the answer is simple; He wants us to have a relationship with Him! It's always been the exact plan of God before the foundation of the earth. Yep, you heard it right, before God created the very Earth you walk on today, He sent His Son to die in our place to have a relationship with Him and communion with Him eternally.

Once Adam sinned, humanity developed a sinful desire which Satan was and still is able to use against us. It's almost like a doggie that can sniff out any food you have on you. That doggie knows there's a treat somewhere in your pocket, he can smell it. Well, likewise Satan our enemy can smell (spiritually) the sin in our lives. He knows our weakness, similar to the way God knows them. The only difference is Satan has no compassion, no grace, and no mercy. He knows what can take away your peace or joy; he is after that! Sin only affects us and the ones around us, when we make bad choices consequences will come and this again hurt us! His goal is to bring as many people with him into eternal damnation. He's going there forever, and He wants you there with Him. This is real, and whoever speaks about Jesus Christianity or the Bible needs to know and believe Satan the enemy is real. They always say that misery loves company right? Well, the enemy wants as much company as He can have. That's why there's a spiritual war going on in the heavens for your soul, even as you are reading right now.

"For we wrestle not against flesh and blood, but against principalities, against powers, against the rulers of the darkness of this world, against spiritual wickedness in high places" (Ephesians 6:12).

It all sounds very scary at first right? Spiritual battles, Satan, and your soul can make your mind uneasy. From a glance, it is scary, until you know who God is and what He's done in our lives. The main battle of our soul eternally and where it goes, well that battle has already been won. It's been won at the cross of Christ.

"Where, O death is your victory? Where, O death is your sting?" The sting of death is sin, and the power of sin is the law. But thanks be to God! He gives us the victory through our Lord Jesus Christ" (1 Corinthians 15:55-57).

See, God in His infinite wisdom, had a plan or a promise. Remember we talked about God's plan, and how Jesus was slain before the foundation of the earth? Well, it wasn't just a plan, it was also a promise.

I am talking about God's faithfulness through His promises! As a matter of fact, God has never broken a promise or failed to deliver on a promise that He's made. Never.

"When God made his promise to Abraham, God gave his word. There was no one greater than himself to promise by. So he promised by making an appeal to himself. He said, "I will certainly bless you. I will give you many children." Abraham was patient while he waited. Then he received what God promised him" (Hebrews 6:13-15).

"All inhabitants of the earth will worship the beast--all whose names have not been written in the Lamb's book of life, the Lamb who was slain from the creation of the world" (*Revelation 13:8).*

See in the book of Revelation; it is written that Jesus died before the world ever began. Our God is called the Alpha and the Omega (The Beginning and the End). Our God is outside of time (very hard for the human mind to comprehend). In His wisdom and love, which was the very reason He formulated this plan in the beginning, He knew our human weaknesses. These weaknesses or sins would lead us away from Him eternally. He knew this before Adam first sinned in the garden, remember this God we are talking about, not your grandfather who forgot where he left his keys. In God's infinite wisdom, He knew once His creation (you and me) had free will, and we would eventually fail, and Adam did just that in the Garden of Eden. Satan then came to Adam in the garden, and this is what he said to Adam:

"Now the serpent was more crafty than any of the wild animals the Lord God had made. He said to the woman, "Did God really say, 'You must not eat from any tree in the garden?" (Genesis 3:1).

What you must realize is that God provided a beautiful garden for Adam with many lush fruit trees and full dominion over all the animals. He just had one request. That request was not to eat from one certain tree.

"And the Lord God commanded the man, "You are free to eat from any tree in the garden; 17 but you must not eat from the tree of the knowledge of good and evil, for when you eat from it you will certainly die." (Genesis 2:1617).

So the Lord openly and transparently explained to Adam what would happen to him if he ate from this tree that Adam would die. At that point, once he disobeyed God's one request, Adam died, first spiritually and then physically. See, physical death is a result of the spiritual death of sin in our lives. Now, remember Adam had a whole garden to enjoy with dominion over all the animals. God just had a very small request; don't eat from the one tree of knowledge of good or evil. Now it's interesting to know that Adam didn't have any interest in eating from that tree until Satan brought the idea to him in the garden. Remember, God created Satan, like an angel. There was a point where Satan thought he was equal to God and at some points greater than God. It was this pride that sent Satan from heaven into this earth for a short season.

He replied, "I saw Satan fall like lightning from heaven" (Luke 10:18).

Jesus said this, and it was recorded in the Gospel of Luke. Satan tempted Adam with something he didn't even want from the beginning. Adam never struggled with the idea of eating from the tree of life until he met Satan in the garden. It's how we find our own lives today. We end up in troubles, addictions, making poor choices trying to fill our voids in our lives all because of Satan's temptations. Sometimes also we get temptations confused with one of God's tests in our lives. It's important to remember that God will never ever tempt us in our lives. That is solely the work of the Devil Satan.

"When tempted, no one should say, "God is tempting me." For God cannot be tempted by evil, nor does he tempt anyone; but each person is tempted when they are dragged away by their own evil desire and enticed. Then, after desire has conceived, it gives birth to sin; and sin, when it is full-grown, gives birth to death" (James 1:13-15).

Chapter Three

Religion & Spirituality

Before we explore the difference between religion and spirituality, we must first define the two terms. Religion can be defined as "the belief in and worship of God or gods, usually expressed in conduct and ritual" or "any specific system of belief, worship, etc., often involving a code of ethics." Spirituality, on the other hand, can be defined as "the quality or fact of being spiritual, non-physical" or "predominantly of spiritual character as shown in thought, life, etc.; spiritual tendency or tone." To put it briefly, religion is a set of beliefs and rituals that claim to get a person in a right relationship with God, while spirituality is a focus on spiritual things and the spiritual world instead of physical or earthly things.

The most common misconception about religion is that Christianity is just another religion like Islam, Judaism, Hinduism, etc. Sadly, many who claim to be adherents of Christianity do practice Christianity as if it were a religion. To many, Christianity is nothing more than a set of rules and rituals that a person has to observe to go to heaven after death. That is not true about Christianity. True Christianity is not a religion; rather, it is having a right relationship with God by receiving Jesus Christ as the Savior-Messiah, by grace through faith. Yes, Christianity does encourage us to get baptized, have communion, but this is more for our faith to grow more in Him. This is a choice for you to get stronger in Him but it does not bring salvation; only accepting Jesus as your Lord and savior will bring eternal life. Yes, Christianity does have "rules" to follow like the Ten Commandments which shows us the basics (e.g., do not murder, love one another, etc.). However, these rituals and rules are not the essence of Christianity. The rituals and rules of Christianity are the sources of salvation. When we receive salvation through Jesus Christ, we are baptized as a proclamation of faith. We observe communion in remembrance of Christ's sacrifice. We also follow a list of dos and don'ts out of love for God and gratitude for what He has done.

The most common misconception about spirituality is that there are many forms of spirituality, and they are all equally and valid. Meditating in unusual physical positions, communing with nature, seeking conversation with the spirit world, etc. may seem to be "spiritual," but they are false spirituality. True spirituality possesses the Holy Spirit of God as a result of receiving salvation through Jesus Christ.

True spirituality is the fruit that the Holy Spirit

produces in a person's life: love, joy, peace, patience, kindness, goodness, faithfulness, gentleness, and self-control (Galatians 5:22-23). Spirituality is all about becoming more like God, who is spirit (John 4:24), and having our character conformed to His image (Romans 12:1-2).

What religion and spirituality have in common is that they both can be false methods of having a relationship with God. Religion tends to substitute the heartless observance of rituals for a genuine relationship with God. Spirituality tends to substitute a connection with the spirit world for a genuine relationship with God. Both can be, and often are, false paths to God. At the same time, religion can be valuable in the sense that it points to the fact that there is a God and that we are somehow accountable to Him. The only true value of religion is its ability to point out that we have fallen short and are in need of a Savior. Spirituality can be valuable in that it points out the fact that the physical world is not all there is. Human beings are not only material but also possess a soul-spirit. There is a spiritual world around us, of which we should be aware. The true value of spirituality is that it points to the fact that there are something and someone beyond this physical world to which we need to connect.

Jesus Christ is the fulfillment of both religion and spirituality. He is the One to whom we are accountable and to whom true religion points. He is the One to whom we need to connect and the One to whom true spirituality points.

To understand this, we need to focus on what God does for us when we accept Jesus Christ as our savior. Let's look at an analogy of an operation! When a surgeon operates on a patient, he incises the diseased area with the help of a knife. Similarly, God performs an "operation" on human beings, though there is no physical incision. God cuts the direct connection between our souls and flesh.

"And Jesus answered them, "Those who are well have no need of a physician, but those who are sick. I have not come to call the righteous but sinners to repentance" (Luke 5:31-32),

"For the word of God is living and active, sharper than any two-edged sword, piercing to the division of soul and of spirit, of joints and of marrow, and discerning the thoughts and intentions of the heart" (Hebrews 4:12)

"Having been buried with him in baptism, in which you were also raised with him through faith in the powerful working of God, who raised him from the dead" (Colossians 2:12)

But a Jew is one inwardly, and circumcision is a matter of the heart, by the Spirit, not by the letter. His praise is not from man but from God. (Romans 2:29)

When you accept this great gift of salvation with faith in the shed blood of Jesus Christ, you will be purified, and you will see great changes in your thoughts and attitude. Your heart will be more inclined to agree with God's commandments, and you will be more spiritual. However, the body may resist and would keep pulling you to the worldly pleasures.

"So I find it to be a law that when I want to do right, evil lies close at hand. For I delight in the law of God, in my inner being, but I see in my members another law waging war against the law of my mind and making me captive to the law of sin that dwells in my members. Wretched man that I am! Who will deliver me from this body of death? Thanks be to God through Jesus Christ our Lord! So then, I myself serve the law of God with my mind, but with my flesh I serve the law of sin"(Romans 7:21-25).

When you embrace Jesus in your life, your soul is reborn and saved, but the physical body may not be saved. The body remains inclined to do evil things, whereas your soul and the spirit condemn those evil things. In fact, your soul and spirit help you to resist all sorts of enticements and inclinations to doing evil acts.

Let's face it; no Christian is flawless in the body. At times, we surrender to our worldly desires, and we sin; but when we have Him, we have remorseful feelings when they have deviated from their righteous path.

"If we say we have no sin, we deceive ourselves, and the truth is not in us"(1 John 1:8)

"My little children, I am writing these things to you so that you may not sin. But if anyone does sin, we have an advocate with the Father, Jesus Christ the righteous" (1 John 2).

In the case of a physical incision in operation by a surgeon, the incised area can't be restored. Similarly, when the body is cut away from the soul, it can't be attached to each other again. We need to realize how great our God is and how He gives the gift of salvation to us and it is for eternity. It is not our good deeds that help us get salvation, but because of the blessings of God to us.

"For all have sinned and fall short of the glory of God.." (Romans 3:23).

"Yet we know that a person is not justified by works of the law but through faith in Jesus Christ, so we also have believed in Christ Jesus, in order to be justified by faith in Christ and not by works of the law, because by works of the law no one will be justified" (Galatians 2:16).

Here, the undeniable truth is that since we can't earn salvation, we can't un-earn it either. Our God is the Master of our souls, so our souls always remain His property, and He does not let His belongings get dirty. He is always pure and will help us stay pure.

When you have embraced Jesus, you are showered by God's love. We don't need to be worried because He will always hold onto us.

"For I am sure that neither death nor life, nor angels nor rulers, nor things present nor things to come, nor powers,39 nor height nor depth, nor anything else in all creation, will be able to separate us from the love of God in Christ Jesus our Lord"
(Romans 8:38-39).

Chapter Four

Can We Control Our Thoughts?

"Keep your heart with all vigilance, for from it flow the springs of life" **(Proverbs 4:23).**

It is crucial that we control our thoughts, no matter how, as we can see its importance in the above verse. They say that when we sin, we do it twice; first in our thoughts, and secondly, when we actually do it. We can get rid of sins if we try and eliminate the thought of sins right in the beginning.

"Finally, brothers, whatever is true, whatever is honorable, whatever is just, whatever is pure, whatever is lovely, whatever is commendable, if there is any excellence, if there is anything worthy of praise, think about these things"(Philippians 4:8).

We have to identify the difference between being tempted when bad thoughts occur and committing sin when we amplify those evil thoughts. The moment an evil thought originates in the mind, we need to see it in light of God's words. This way helps reject evil thoughts and replace them with good ones. If you are already in the habit of giving enough time to develop thoughts in mind, it will turn out to be tougher to influence the thought process. One of the best ways to get rid of evil thoughts is to know God's Word that will help you take control of your thoughts. This has helped me in my walk with Christ. When you have God's words in mind, you can quickly identify a bad thought and take steps to prevent it. To understand this, we need to be born again; if not, we will continue with our rebellious thoughts and actions, thinking there are no consequences of anything.

Satan is our open enemy, and it leaves no opportunity to tempt us, which he even did so to Jesus. But Satan can never overpower our savior. Jesus countered Satan's temptations with biblical verses.

"Then Jesus was led up by the Spirit into the wilderness to be tempted by the devil. And after fasting forty days and forty nights, he was hungry. And the tempter came and said to him, "If you are the Son of God, command these stones to become loaves of bread." But he answered, "It is written, "'Man shall not live by bread alone, but by every word that comes from the mouth of God.'" Then the devil took him to the holy city and set him on the pinnacle of the temple and said to him, "If you are the Son of God, throw yourself down, for it is written, "'He will command his angels concerning you,' And

"'On their hands they will bear you up, lest you strike your foot against a stone.'" Jesus said to him, "Again it is written, 'You shall not put the Lord your God to the test.'" Again, the devil took him to a very high mountain and showed him all the kingdoms of the world and their glory. And he said to him, "All these I will give you, if you will fall down and worship me." Then Jesus said to him, "Be gone, Satan! For it is written, "'You shall worship the Lord your God and him only shall you serve.'" Then the devil left him, and behold, angels came and were ministering to him"(Matthew 4).

You can see here how Jesus countered every word of temptation offered by Satan. So, if you refer to the Bible at the time of being tempted, you will be saved for sure. However, you need to know some verses, especially of God's promises, to prevent temptations. Every bad choice we make will have a consequence that is either going to hurt us or someone we love.

When we realize that sin only satisfies us for a season but doesn't completely fulfill the will of God in us, we will change the way we think.

To do this, the best way is to read the word of God with a focus on its meanings. See, temptation starts from a thought. Jesus said that when we commit adultery, it starts in our hearts because we did not control or rebuke that thought and that's why it came down to our hearts, and that's when we need to take ourselves to the cross for forgiveness. We do not commit adultery when we touch the person or see the person in secrete or sleep with the person. Adultery actually occurs when we let it grow in our thoughts and let it enter our hearts and because of this, our relationship with our spouse changes negatively. That is why our thoughts are very important as they affect all we are doing. That is why we need to know that our thought is key in our walk of faith.

We know ourselves very well, and therefore, ought to know the things that are most tempting to us; things like anger, greed, pride, vanity, selfishness, lust, etc. There are hundreds of biblical verses that discourage these negative feelings. We need to read, and preferably memorize, and practice verses relevant to your temptations and the ones that tell the rewards of saving yourself from those temptations. The moment a temptation attacks you, all need to do is recall those verses, and you will indeed be saved. To control our thoughts, we need to learn how to live, depending on the Holy Spirit, and ask for help through prayers because we are weak. Bringing our sins and thoughts to the light will help us get deeper into a Godly life. Having the right people in your life to confess these things to is key to a successful Godly life.

"Watch and pray that you may not enter into temptation. The spirit indeed is willing, but the flesh is weak" (Matthew 26:41).

"Whoever trusts in his own mind is a fool, but he who walks in wisdom will be delivered" (Proverbs 28:26)

"The heart is deceitful above all things, and desperately sick; who can understand it?" (Jeremiah 17:9)

(Proverbs 4:23) tells us clearly that we must stay away from everything that can cause evil thoughts.

"But put on the Lord Jesus Christ, and make no provision for the flesh, to gratify its desires" (Romans 13:14).

In light of the above verse, we are supposed to stay away from all forms of bad habits and content in magazines, videos, websites, talks, and circumstances that can lead us to sin. And also people whose company can lead us into sin. I mean wherever our heart is, we are to seek for the best place we can have Him, His word and love as the best choices to make.

We are in this world to follow God's words, so we must replace all sinful things with holy pursuits. We have to follow this replacement principle of evil with good.

"But I say to you, Love your enemies and pray for those who persecute you.."(Matthew 5:44)

"Let the thief no longer steal, but rather let him labor, doing honest work with his own hands, so that he may have something to share with anyone in need" *(Ephesians 4:28).*

If lust overcomes your thoughts, turn away your gaze, and admire how God has made us beautiful beings. And say prayers for the woman or man that she or he finds God and be on the righteous path. Consider other women or men as your mothers, fathers and sisters or brothers. If insecurities come or rejection thoughts come, remind yourself that you are unique and special, and all that matters is that God loves you.

"Older women as mothers, younger women as sisters, in all purity"(1 Timothy 5:2).

As you go through biblical verses, you will notice that we are asked to abstain from bad deeds and ideas, but it is not enough to keep your soul clean. If you are successful at throwing bad thoughts away, you empty your mind. If your mind remains empty, it is still at high risk of being attacked by Satan. Thus, you will not only need to empty your mind but also fill it in with good thoughts to stay safe against temptations.

"Therefore, having put away falsehood, let each one of you speak the truth with his neighbor, for we are members one of another. Be angry and do not sin; do not let the sun go down on your anger, and give no opportunity to the devil. Let the thief no longer steal, but rather let him labor, doing honest work with his own hands, so that he may have something to share with anyone in need. Let no corrupt talk come out of your mouth, but only such as is good for building up, as fits the occasion, that it may give grace to those who hear. And do not grieve the Holy Spirit of God, by whom you were sealed for the day of redemption. Let all bitterness and wrath and anger and clamor and slander be put away from you, along with all malice. Be kind to one another, tenderhearted, forgiving one another, as God in Christ forgave you" *(Ephesians 4:22-32)*.

Another way to control your thoughts is to bond with other Christians, as God wants us to have good relationships with others. The good influence in your circle can help you adopt the good changes you wish to bring in your thoughts, attitude, and personality.

The people who pray for us and with us with sincerity and help us avoid bad ways are certainly the best friends we can ever have.

"And let us consider how to stir up one another to love and good works, 25 not neglecting to meet together, as is the habit of some, but encouraging one another, and all the more as you see the Day drawing near" (Hebrews 10:24-25).

These ways will work when you have faith in Christ as Savior and have sincere intention to get rid of sins.

With no sincerity and honesty, you may not experience good outcomes. Our Lord is gracious and forgiving, but we must honor Him with what matters to Him. We need to match our outside appearance and intentions with our inside.

Chapter Five

Worshipping Our Thoughts or Our King?

When we say worship, it means to show reverence and adoration for God. Why is it so important to worship God? The way we defeat the battlefield we have in our minds is by spending our time wisely reading and seeing the right things.

I can't express enough how important this is for me. In fact, this part is my favorite part of this book, and I am so grateful to God that I can share it. Worshipping God every day has allowed me to grow so much in my identity with Christ.

This has allowed me to be closer to Him by putting my focus on Him more than myself. This has also helped me control my thoughts and insecurities. It is something I can't explain, and it feels like a supernatural phenomenon to me. My heart is softer towards Him and others when I worship Him. Worship for me is like talking to God. There are so many great songs, worship bands, and groups. They seem to be infinite! Even if on some days, it doesn't feel like doing it, you do it based on obedience, and I promise you that it will change your day, your ways, and your entire being. It is a must to worship, not just one time a week, but every day and possibly every time you have during the day.

You simply have to make up your mind and decide who you are, who you are choosing to serve, if you are choosing to serve yourself, you will listen to songs that will bring you to emotional past, a loss or even deception. If you are choosing to worship Him, you will never be wrong. Listening to His Word through songs will help you grow your faith because faith comes by hearing the word of God. Also, when you don't know what to pray, listening to worship is a way to communicate with Him.

Come on, Jesus saves us from Hell and this dark world! Everyone, it is time to wake up and have a revival in our hearts and minds. It is my goal for you to believe it's not over when you die! Praising Him is an honor and not a sacrifice. Listening to the right things in songs has given me strength and has changed my mind. Instead of thinking about temporary things, I constantly think about eternal things, and this allows me to always walk with Him in His spirit, love, joy, and peace.

"God is spirit, and those who worship him must worship in spirit and truth" (John

4:24).

There is nothing more important than to hear about Him and His heart for you. We were made to worship Him. Any other songs we hear are nice, but the message in those songs is so temporary. God is real, and the sanctification that God wants for your life as you listen to His songs is real if you seek Him! When we hear about Him in music, our ears connect with our mind and our mind with our heart and our heart with our spirit. They all make us stronger. When sin and temptation come, we can reject, and it is all about training our minds to hear the right things and saying NO to the things our conscience feels uncomfortable.

I included some verses to help you connect with Him in worship;

"Go to the LORD for help, and worship him continually" (1 Chronicle 16:11).

"His love is eternal" (Psalm 118:4).

"Addressing one another in psalms and hymns and spiritual songs, singing and making melody to the Lord with your heart, giving thanks always and for everything to God the Father in the name of our Lord Jesus Christ" (Ephesians 5:19-20)

"I appeal to you therefore, brothers, by the mercies of God, to present your bodies as a living sacrifice, holy and acceptable to God, which is your spiritual worship. Do not be conformed to this world, but be transformed by the renewal of your mind, that by testing You may discern what is the will of God what is good and acceptable and perfect"(Romans 12:1-2).

"Praise the Lord our God; worship before his throne! Holy is he!" (Psalm 99:5)

"Lord, you are my God; I will exalt you and praise your name, for in perfect faithfulness You have done wonderful things, things planned long ago" (Isaiah 25:1).

"Sing to the Lord; praise the Lord! For he has delivered the life of the needy from the hand of evildoers" (Jeremiah 20:13).

Because our battlefield is in our minds, we have to constantly battle our thoughts, and the easiest way to do it is to turn on your radio in the house or your iPhone and start enjoying listening to Godly songs. God says that whatever is in your mind; that's who you are! There is power in your thoughts. The battlefield again is in our minds.

When we worship, when we sing to God, when our ears constantly hear His songs, made and written by believers who have experienced His presence, our soul heals, our mind gets renewed, and our spirit gets stronger. See, God is LOVE so if we seek Him daily His love will overflow our hearts! Worshiping the name of the Lord Jesus is a necessity a must and a need in everyone's life! When our minds and hearts discovered the meaning of this new life, we will start meditating on new and positive thoughts as well we will start pouring out a new love for others. King David mentioned some good and strong reasons to praise and worship our God:

"Who made heaven and earth, the sea, and all that is in them, who keeps faith forever; Who executes justice for the oppressed, who gives food to the hungry? The Lord sets the prisoners free; The Lord opens the eyes of the blind. The Lord lifts up those who are bowed down; the Lord loves the righteous. The Lord watches over the sojourners; he upholds the widow and the fatherless, but the way of the wicked he brings to ruin.

The Lord will reign forever, your God, O Zion, to all generations. Praise the Lord!" **(Psalm 146:6-10)**

It is crucial that everyone understands again that we are in a spiritual battle. There is no way to get out of it. Awareness of the spiritual battle around us is very important. Not only awareness, but vigilance, preparedness, courage, and the right weaponry are crucial elements of engaging in spiritual warfare. In the words of Paul in (2 Corinthians 10:3–5), "For though we walk in the flesh, we do not war according to the flesh, for the weapons of our warfare are not of the flesh, but divinely powerful for the destruction of fortresses. We are destroying speculations and every lofty thing raised against the knowledge of God. We are taking every thought captive to the obedience of Christ." It is clear that "our warfare" as Christians is spiritual. We are not fighting a physical battle or a human battle. It is on a spiritual level—its enemies, its prerogatives, its fortresses, and its weapons are all spiritual. If we attempt to fight the spiritual with human weapons, we will fail and the enemy will be victorious.

It is important to note that Paul is not speaking about battling demons here. When Jesus and the apostles cast demons out, it was, along with the other signs and wonders they exhibited, primarily to prove the authority of what they said. It was important at that time for God to give the apostles a powerful "proof" that they were indeed from God and His spokesmen. The fidelity of Scripture depends on the authority of the apostles, so God gave the apostles His power to authenticate their teachings. The point all along was to show that the ultimate authority and our ultimate spiritual weapon is Scripture. The kind of spiritual battle that every Christian engages in is primarily a battle of the mind and heart.

The spiritual battle is quite personal for each Christian. The devil is like a "roaring lion" seeking to devour, and we must remain vigilant against him (1Peter 5:8). The enemy of our souls has "flaming arrows" that can only be extinguished by the shield of faith as handled by a believer equipped with the full armor of God (Ephesians 6:10–17). Jesus told us to "watch and pray" so as not to fall into temptation (Mark 14:38).

According to (2 Corinthians 10:4–5), there are spiritual fortresses in this world made of the "speculations" and "lofty things." The word speculations are, in the Greek, logismos. It means "ideas, concepts, reasoning, and philosophies." People of the world build up these logismos to protect themselves against the truth of God. Sadly, these fortresses often become prisons and eventually tombs. As Christians, we have a calling to break down these fortresses and rescue the inhabitants. It is dangerous and difficult work, but we have a divine arsenal always at our disposal. Unfortunately, one of the enemy's best tricks is getting us to fight with human weapons rather than divine.

When fighting against worldly philosophies,

human wit and weaponry are of no avail. Marketing techniques, counter-philosophies, persuasive words of human wisdom (1 Corinthians 2:4), rationalism, organization, skill, entertainment, mystique, better lighting, better music—these are all human weapons. None of these things will win the spiritual war. The only effective thing—the only offensive weapon we possess—is the Sword of the Spirit, which is the Word of God (Ephesians 6:17). This sword gives us many freedoms as soldiers in this spiritual battle. We have freedom from fear, knowing that God is fighting for us (Joshua 1:7–9) and that He will not forsake us. We have freedom from guilt, knowing that we are not responsible for the souls of those who reject God's message after we have proclaimed it to them (Mark 6:11). We have freedom from despair, knowing that, if we are persecuted and hated, Christ was persecuted and hated first (John 15:18) and that our battle wounds will be richly and lovingly tended to in heaven (Matthew 5:10).

All of these freedoms come from using the powerful weapon of God His Words. If we use human weapons to fight the temptations of the wicked one, we will sustain failures and disappointment.

Conversely, the victories of God are full of hope. **"Let us draw near with a sincere heart in full assurance of faith, having our hearts sprinkled clean from an evil conscience, and our bodies**

washed with pure water. Let us hold fast the confession of our hope without wavering, for He who promised is faithful" (Hebrews10:22-23). The hearts of those who hear and accept the true, full message of the gospel as given by the apostles are "sprinkled clean" and "washed with pure water." What is this water? It is the Word of God that strengthens us as we fight (Ephesians 5:26; John 7:38).

Chapter Six

Why on Earth Do Bad Things Happen?

The world we are living in has lots of sufferings and pain to offer us. I don't see even a single soul that is not undergoing or has already endured some sort of suffering. Everyone, queens and kings, rich and poor, we all have emotions, feelings, and brains! There are many harsh realities in this world, and they raise the following question:

"Why do bad things happen?"

It is, in fact, one of the toughest questions in theology. Since God is answerable to none, everything that happens must have been permitted by Him, if they are not caused by Him directly. First of all, we must admit that we are not everlasting or all-knowing beings, and we can't expect ourselves or our minds to comprehend God's ways of doing things completely. Thus, we sometimes are unable to understand when things do not go in our favor. Well, to find an answer, we can see the book of Job with the question of "why bad things happen."

Again Job was a virtuous man. However, he suffered in many unimaginable ways. God permitted Satan to try his all tricks on Job other than killing him, and Satan played his worst tricks. Every time, Job's reaction was submissive to God. He said:

"Though he slay me, I will hope in him; yet I will argue my ways to his face" (Job 13:15).

Though Job was puzzled why God permitted Satan to do those things, he knew in his heart that God was gracious, and Job never ceased to trust Him. There is great learning for us in Job's reaction that whatever God does never occurs without reason. His plans are the best, and He tests us through trials and sufferings so that we grow in faith. We need to understand that we are not "good." In fact, we are stained with sin.

"Surely there is not a righteous man on earth who does good and never sins" (Ecclesiastes 7:20)

"For all have sinned and fall short of the glory of God" (Romans 3:23).

"If we say we have no sin, we deceive ourselves, and the truth is not in us" (1 John 1:8).

"No one is good—except God alone" (Luke 18:19).

We all feel the effects of committing sins in some manner. Sometimes, it is our own sins and sometimes of others' sins. Do you know that we live in a fallen world? Thus, we face the effects of the fall. Among these effects, there is injustice, prejudice, and apparently suffering that sometimes makes no sense to us.

When you think why God allows bad things to happen to us, you also need to reflect on a few other things. First of all, bad things do happen to good people. But do you think this world is the end? Of course, not! As Christians, we have an everlasting viewpoint, so we can never lose our hearts and our hope. It seems that time affects our body, and indeed it is only our body that time can damage. We are renewed with every passing day as we get closer and closer to meet our maker. Our temporary difficulties takes us closer to our eternal glory that outweighs all problems. Thus, we have to pay attention to the unseen because that is eternal.

"So we do not lose heart. Though our outer self is wasting away, our inner self is being renewed day by day. For this light momentary affliction is preparing for us an eternal weight of

glory beyond all comparison, as we look not to the things that are seen but to the things that are unseen. For the things that are seen are transient, but the things that are unseen are eternal" (2 Corinthians 4:16-18).

We know that we would be rewarded gloriously. When bad things happen to us, we thank God because God would reward us with great and lasting rewards.

"And we know that for those who love God all things work together for good, for those who are called according to his purpose" (Romans 8:28).

"But Joseph said to them, "Do not fear, for am I in the place of God? As for you, you meant evil against me, but God meant it for good, to bring it about that many people should be kept alive, as they are today. So do not fear; I will provide for you and your little ones." Thus, he comforted them and spoke kindly to them" (Genesis 50:19–21).

When bad things happen to people, it becomes a way of strengthening their faith and trust in God.

"Blessed be the God and Father of our Lord Jesus Christ, the Father of mercies and God of all comfort, who comforts us in all our affliction,

so that we may be able to comfort those who are in any affliction, with the comfort with which we ourselves are comforted by God. For as we share abundantly in Christ's sufferings, so through Christ we share abundantly in comfort too" *(2 Corinthians 1:3-5).*

Jesus is above us all, yet he suffered more than we can ever imagine. He suffered for us and shed his blood for our sins. We have to follow his footsteps.

"For what credit is it if, when you sin and are beaten for it, you endure? But if when you do good and suffer for it you endure, this is a gracious thing in the sight of God. For to this, you have been called, because Christ also suffered for you, leaving you an example, so that you might follow in his steps. He committed no sin, neither was deceit found in his mouth. When he was reviled, he did not revile in return; when he suffered, he did not threaten, but continued entrusting himself to him who judges justly" *(1 Peter 2:20–23).*

So, Jesus endured pain and (**Romans 5:8**) tells us, **"but God shows his love for us in that while we were still sinners, Christ died for us."** In spite of our sinful nature, God does not hesitate to show His love for us. Hence, we will be forgiven if we embrace Jesus as our savior.

When bad things happen, God has a reason

that we may not understand in the time of our difficulties. When we believe in God, we know that He is merciful, just, and loving. In place of suspecting God's ways, we react in a way that shows our trust in Him.

"Trust in the Lord with all your heart and do not lean on your own understanding. In all your ways acknowledge him, and he will make straight your paths" (Proverbs 3:5–6).

Chapter Seven

My Story

There was a time in my life I was bound to please others. I was a follower, not a leader until I turned 25. This was when I gave my life, my heart, my time, and my thoughts to Christ. I gave myself a chance to try God and His Word like never before. This was God's timing; I was ready. I felt there was something more in life than just eat, work, have fun, and think about myself. I was tired of living life on my own or depending on others like my Dad, boyfriends or friends. I was just empty, searching for more than my own selfish desires.

Yes, I enjoyed and had fun in this world, had great friends, great jobs and was very popular, but like the Word of God said; sin only lasts for a season, I am not saying that working, having friends, and going out is a sin; what I am trying to say is inside of me, I knew I needed to find myself.

I knew there was more for me in this life than what I already knew, which was not fulfilling and did not have eternal rewards. I was tired of the pattern of life lived in this world; I never felt I fit. I always felt out of place. Never had that sense of belonging of worth. I wanted to be freely me and God knew this. Can you believe that He Knew I was ready for this new life I have for myself now? Yes, we will all have that time when we make this kind of decision, which is the most important decision you will ever make in your life. Before Him, I had no identity, and that is why I was a follower. I was trapped trying to please everyone but God.

I tried to copy the things I thought were good, but they were sins that were hurting others and me as well. I tried to please my friends and the people around me by watching the wrong programs and movies on TV, which emotionally made me the person I was. This created fear and insecurities in my life. Losing my brother and mother at such a young age and living with a father who yet didn't had the relationship he has with God today, was difficult because his identity was in his wealth. This made everything more difficult for me to understand God.

There is no one to blame or nothing to regret because we will all taste and experience the grieving of this world, which is so temporary. But this condition affected me deeply, that's why I put my identity in the people around me and the things I saw around me. I was confused and started to search for attention and love in the wrong places. Making the wrong choices, I started getting connected with the wrong people. Is so true what God's word says about this in: (**1** *Corinthians 15:33 NLT*)

"Don't be fooled by those who say such things, for bad company corrupts good character."

I knew I needed balance in my life, balance to invest more time feeding my spirit than my flesh, and all my desires. I made my decision to start getting to know my creator at 25 years of age. That is when things started changing in my life! My pride, ego, my old identity, and judgment started leaving me, even my hard heart started softening and I started standing up for the truth of His purity, having the identity I needed to have in Christ.

The way we judge others is the same way we will be judged. God's word said it this way in; **(Matthew 7:1-5NLT)**

Do Not Judge Others

"Do not judge others, and you will not be judged. For you will be treated as you treat others. The standard you use in judging is the standard by which you will be judged. And why worry about a speck in your friend's eye when you have a log in your own? How can you think of saying to your friend, Let me help you get rid of that speck in your eye,' when you can't see past the log in your own eye? Hypocrite! First get rid of the log in your

own eye; then you will see well enough to deal with the speck in your friend's eye.

We have to be careful the way we see others, our looks, the way we dress, the color of our skin, our financial status and our beauty. I have to remind myself that we are dust, and we will go to dust. I also have to remind myself that God just doesn't love me but everyone in this world! That love letter I shared with you on the beginning of this book is not just for you or me but for every single human being in the face of this world!

Making fun of others, judging them, demeaning them, rejecting them, and abandoning them is not the right thing to do, but a problem. Making false witness against others is strictly forbidden in one of the commandments, but we find ourselves doing these things every day instead of praying. Someone prayed for me, and I was found. Someone who already knew God was able to teach me and be there for me so that I could see myself in Him. This healed my heart and soul and renewed my mind so I could treat others and myself the way God desires.

Pleasing others will make you believe that sin is OK, and there are no consequences of doing it. I express this to all the young girls out there who are people-pleasers. Because if we don't follow the real

Leader, the real Hero Jesus Christ and His Word, the reality and truth about God's Word, we will miss out on the peace and purpose He has for our lives. We will be confused, just wondering and making the wrong choices or just conforming, not transforming. Why should I be pleasing people who are not offering me eternity?

I please God by believing in the truth of His pure words; that's who we need to worship and adore. When we worship Him, He gives us more of His favor, of His grace, stability, and purpose. Our God is in control of everything. The best thing that happened to me was I got rid of all anxiety, and I started really praying and trusting who is in complete control of my life, who knows my beginning and my ending. Beauty comes from the inside. He wants us to understand that charm is deceitful and beauty is passing, but whoever fears the Lord shall be praised and will be honored. Beauty comes from a quiet, modest, and gentle spirit, and in His presence, and there is the fullness of joy.

I needed to feel the emptiness of this life to understand what I was living and experiencing with Him, and clearly saw how God rescued me, how all I needed was for Him to fill me! I needed to be that prodigal daughter and fall deep to be able to see and feel the difference between both of my lives. I now find my identity in Christ, my morality values, and conscience are all in His hands, and He perfects them daily.

I have met the most wonderful people. I have grown so much in His love and Word, which has put my trust and faith only in Him.

If I do not have Him, I would be fearful and would not be able to handle problems as I do now without emotions. With love, I see others and this world the way God sees it, instead of the way I want to see things. Isn't it beautiful to know people and love them for who they are? Yes, when we are close to Him, all things are possible! And all we care about is hearing and loving others. My passion is encourage others to share their stories and their life testimonies because this will draw them closer to Him.

We have to discipline ourselves to persevere in doing good deeds. If I did not love myself, how could I love others? To love yourself, you have to know who you are in Him and discover your purpose and gifts, and then He will give you an identity.

Is your identity based on others? In your job? In your degree? In your friends? In your beauty? The way you dress? In your age? Is your identity in your struggles? Are you going to continue to be labeled by others? Or by God?

His Word is what will bring us face to face

with our real identity. See, the problem starts when others label your identity. Jealousy, bitterness, pride, ego, hypocrisy, etc. will not leave you easily. You will not be able to please everyone. Quite the opposite, all those emotions will define you.

However, if God labels you, He will change you from the inside out. He will bring all those beautiful and pure things He made in you, and your uniqueness will be exposed, and this is how your freedom will come. See, when there is no identity of yours, anything in life will influence you because you will see and hear the wrong voices, and you will not be able to recognize them. If your conscience does, you will not obey, because you will not have the power of the Holy Spirit to help you.

You need to acknowledge that you are powerless, and you need help to increase your faith in God. I promise, if you do this, you will be contagious in a Godly way. While I was writing this, I was listening to the song "You alone can rescue by Matt Redman." This is because He rescued me! He rescued me from this dark world, and this dark generation. He rescued me from following things that have no purpose in my life, from my negative thoughts, from my poor decisions, and He sanctifies me every day. That is why I say that listening to Christian Godly songs and worshiping Him will help you start understanding Him. I pray that all of you may hear this message and apply it in your life. Encouragement is what I needed, and I found it in His word and His people. Another great song that I often listen to, to keep my faith growing in Him is by Landon Gingerich.

This song beautifully describes how we make efforts to obtain worldly pleasures whereas God has already great plans for us. All we need to do is keep our faith strongly in Him. The song goes like this:

*This year's felt like four seasons of winter
And you'd give anything you think to feel the sun
Always reaching, always climbing Always
second-guessing the timing But God has a plan,
a purpose in this You are His child so don't you
forget*

He put that hunger in your heart He put that fire in your soul His love is the reason To keep on believing When you feel like giving up When you feel like giving in His love is the reason To keep on believing If we could pull back the curtain of Heaven We would see His hand on everything Every hour Every minute Every second He's always been in it Don't let a shadow of a doubt take hold Hold on to what you already know He put that hunger in your heart He put that fire in your soul His love is the reason To keep on believing When you feel like giving up When you feel like giving in His love is the reason

To keep on believing It's the reason
It's the reason His love is the reason He's the peace in the madness That you can't explain He's the hope in the heartbreak The rest in the suffering He's closer than the air you breathe From the start to the end to the in-between Don't you dare doubt even for a minute What He started in you Yeah, He'sgonna finish!

Reason lyrics © Centricity Music Publishing, FORTYHOURDAYS, COOLNASTY unspoken

Marriage

I met my husband at a church called Calvary Chapel Fort Lauderdale in the year 2008. This was three years after I gave my life to Christ. My husband and I were so deeply involved Christians at that time. We were both crazy in love with Jesus. We would seek Him every day, and our love for Him connected us in a much stronger way. We were so happy to find a place where we really understood Christ's love and to receive the freedom He always wanted for us.

My husband was my best friend, my first

Christian friend. We talked for hours on the phone and shared many of our stories. Everything we talked about was what God was doing in our lives as new believers. Our date nights were going to Christian concerts or conferences and different churches.

I was still healing so many past hurts and relationships, and I did not want to involve myself in a relationship so fast. However, God gave me to love again, my husband. As time passed by, we became closer but always with Jesus. We tried to obey God because we love Him, and we wanted to do things in the right way.

He was always there for me to listen to me and to encourage me with God's word. I was very transparent about my past, and he tried to be transparent with me too. Isn't this the best way to find someone who loves God and fears him? Isn't it wonderful to marry your best friend?

God delivered my husband of so much before we met. He has a story of his own that one day we will share in more detail. He went to the Calvary house, which is a Christian rehab, an amazing ministry for anyone who struggles with codependence or any addiction. He was there for two years, then worked at church and attended Celebrate Recovery.

We both came from broken families, had little

encouragement, and no identity. I lost my mom and my brother when I was just 10 and 12 years old. So, for me, it was hard not having them. Christ's identity was not in me at that time either.

When I became a believer, all I wanted was to marry a Christian man after many broken relationships and empty life. So, this testimony is pretty awesome because when we become closer to God, we think we will get less hurt, but that's not true. What happens is that we still get hurt, but we handle this not in an emotional way but Godly way, and that's all that changes. Jesus never said we would never have turbulences.

My husband and I were friends for two years before we got married. We had a good foundation both in the same faith. We served at church and went to different classes, and we really understood each other. He knew all my past, and I knew his. We tried our best to be as transparent as possible before we got married.

I thought that marrying a Christian was going to be better, maybe perfect, but it was not the case. This is for every Christian woman out there. I thought I was going to get hurt less, but nothing rather happened. Again God will always continue to mold us to become more like Him in loving others. When we think they do not deserve OUR LOVE, He helps us see them as He sees them and He helped me see Rob the way He sees Him.

During the 4th year of my marriage, I found out he was not healed of many things like I wasn't either. Every marriage struggles with this! We think we know our spouse perfectly as no one else does, but that is not true. It is only God who knows everything about our spouses, and that is why we go to Him in prayer when we feel something is not right. Even with all the classes, we took and healing restoration programs, and serving God at church, we still needed more of His restoration and love. This song reminded me of what I was feeling:

Fighting for Me by Riley Clemmons

I need the kinda love that
Can outlast the night
I need the kinda love that
Is willing to fight

When the going gets tough
And my strength's not enough
I see you showing up like never before
This battle for my heart
You took on from the start
You are the peace when my mind's at war
And o-ohh

You will never stop fighting for me
When I can't fight for myself
Every word is a promise you keep
Cause you love me like nobody else

You stand up for me
In the darkest night
When my faith is weak
You're still by my side
You will never stop fighting for me
You will never stop fighting for me

In the perfect timing
You make all things right
You paint a silver lining
In this heart of mine

When the going gets tough
And my strength's not enough
I see you showing up like never before
This battle for my heart
You took on from the start
   You are the peace when my mind's at war
And o-ohh

You will never stop fighting for me
When I can't fight for myself

Every word is a promise you keep
Cause you love me like nobody else

You stand up for me
In the darkest night
When my faith is weak
You're still by my side
You will never stop fighting for me
You will never stop fighting for me

Your love
Is winning me over
Your heart
Is pulling me closer
Your love
Is winning me over
Your heart Is pulling me
closer

You will never stop...
Fighting for me, fighting for me
Every word is a promise you keep, oh, o-
ohh

You will never stop fighting for me
When I can't fight for myself (when I can't)
Every word is a promise you keep (oh, oh)
Cause you love me like nobody else (nobody)

You stand up for me (You stand up for me)
In the darkest night (In the darkest night)
When my faith is weak (yeah, yeah)
You're still by my side (my side)

You will never stop fighting for me (You will never stop)
You will never stop fighting for me!

Source:Musixmatch
Songwriters: Jordan Sapp / Riley Clemmons / Ethan Hulse Fighting for Me lyrics © Be Essential Songs

    While we were in our best years, we were hurting each other and God. We had constant fights and emotional behaviors towards one another. This hurt him and me too. Because of this and because of not being healed, he continued his addictions without letting me know. Lies started to rise, and that is a negative behavior that God needed to bring to an end.

    I prayed, and that is what we do in every circumstance because God is alive, real, and at constant work in our lives. God was faithful and answered. He will always help you! While I was in a very difficult time in my life, I was having an awesome adventure with Jesus at the same time. The peace He gives you when you make decisions is when you know you are hearing from Him and doing His will, trusting Him. This brings joy because faith moves mountains and HIS FAVOR ENCOUNTERS MIRACLES!

I continued to seek Him and helping others seek what is good. I helped my friends to get closer to Him. I continue serving at church, and every lesson I thought was about God's grace and forgiveness. He was teaching me and showing me His heart. He was teaching me that we are all prodigal sons and daughters. See, many stayed in a relationship based on fear or insecurities, but God does not want us to stay in a marriage that way. He wants to continually work to heal un-forgiveness, rejection, hurt, and offense. At that time, my mind was busy with Him. God was using me because I was willing, and even in my hurt, I was obedient. Obedience brings peace that surpasses all understanding.

Sometimes, it is hard to be obedient, but His rewards are amazing and real!

God spoke and said let him work in my husband, and He also wanted to work in me. God said in my spirit that He wanted me to see Rob every week because He wanted to teach me the consequences of sin and that me seeing my husband weekly was a testimony of His grace and mercy. See we tend to share our stories when good things happen but not when bad ones happened knowing that the bad ones will lift God when the good times come our way! That is why it is so important to wisely share, so when things get better God gets all the glory and we can touch hearts and lead them to a different level of faith in Him.

He works quickly when we are seeking him and letting go. When He takes control, time flies! I never stayed quiet. I shared my story, always asking for prayer and guidance, and I was never isolated. I healed and understood that this was not about me. Insecurities and rejection came, but with Him, I overcame them. This means I did not act on my emotions, my rejection, my fears, but I waited to make any decision. I could have said or made many poor choices and end my marriage, but God wanted to create a testimony of marriage in our lives.

To all my readers, we need to be Jesus' hands, ears, mouth, and feet! Of course, I wanted to help but letting God do His thing would bring better results. We just have to learn to trust in His timing. God is never late and never early but always on time. This song reminds me to always love in any circumstances. It is important to love as God loves, and wait patiently for His perfect timing:

The Proof of Your Love

for KING & COUNTRY

If I sing but don't have love
I waste my breath with every song
I bring an empty voice, a hollow noise
If I speak with a silver tongue
Convince a crowd but don't have love
I leave a bitter taste with every word I say

So let my life be the proof,
The proof of your love
Let my love look like you and what you're made
of how you lived, how you died
Love is sacrifice
So let my life be the proof,
The proof of your love

If I give to a needy soul but don't have love then who is poor? It seems all the poverty is found in me so let my life be the proof, The proof of your love Let my love look like you and what you're made of how you lived, how you died

Love is sacrifice
Oh, let my life be the proof,
the proof of your love when it's all said and done
When we sing our final song
Only love remains only love remains
Let my life be the proof, the proof of your love

Let my love look like you and what you're made of how you lived, how you died
Love is sacrifice so let my life be the proof,

The proof of your love!

Source: LyricFind
***Proof of Your Love* lyrics ©**
Warner Chappell Music, Inc

Also, this verse helped me understand what God meant about His timing: **"He has made everything beautiful in His time."**

When you know Jesus and you go back in your sin, it is a lot harder because you know the truth and you have already felt His peace, hope, and joy, and you have heard the truth. It is not good to feel condemned or feel guilty when we sin, but it is ok to feel conviction because of our love for Him. This is hard for everyone that has felt God's presence, peace, true joy, and freedom! However, God is always working in perfecting us.

Loving others instead of revenging is what makes us different, surely, when we do this, people see Jesus in us. Only people who have Christ in them, who fully trust Him, who can hear God, even when they see the worst, are the ones who really walk by faith and not by sight, the ones who instead of being hurt or revenge, love. Only God did this in my heart, and He gets the glory. We will all have to exercise all that we learned in our walk with Him. When situations come, we need to take his word in action. God's word said it this way: **(Philippians 4:9 NIV)**

"Whatever you have learned or received or heard from me, or seen in me—put it into practice. And the God of peace will be with you."

This was the beginning of the restoration season for a broken marriage, and this testimony was one of the ways God used. God also allowed people to see your circumstances like your family and friends because He always has a plan with everything. To fulfill this plan, we need to see the good and the ugly. This is for everything in life. In addition, to learn our lesson, we have to testify about the blessings and the curse.

This was just about some work He needed to do in both of us and through us!

I was not expecting him to change, but I did only what I could do, and it is to change myself. God changed me to have more identity in Him. I was really encountering a God who forgave all of my sins. This was the key to forgive my husband. This is how we need to be with everyone. See, we need to be filled with Jesus, God's word, and His Holy Spirit to understand this.

"Love is patient, love is kind. It does not envy, it does not boast, it is not proud. It does not dishonor others, it is not self-seeking, it is not easily angered, it keeps no record of wrongs. Love does not delight in evil but rejoices with the truth. It always protects, always trusts, always hopes, always perseveres" *(1 Corinthians 13:4-7).*

Today 10 years later, He has given us a different level of grace and faith and love because of what we went through, yet we are imperfect people. We can say we have a lot more of His peace, His joy, His purpose, and His hope. Our minds and hearts have changed; they have become more submissive to His word. The Lord has allowed this to happen in my life to teach me that He is the one who will show me anything that I must know. It is not my place to find out things! My responsibility is to have God's word and LOVE in my heart, always. There is no condemnation for those in Christ. We do not have to feel guilty or condemned anymore at all. He has forgiven us already, so do not ignore God and communicate your struggles and difficulties to Him every day.

Everyone around us was touched. Again, God restores the years that the locust ate, and He does a quick work when you are close to Him. The best blessing God gave us is a transparent, friendly relationship, in which we peacefully resolve our issues and arguments.

I also learned to serve and love my husband more than myself, that it is not about me, but it is about us. See "God cannot be mocked." Even with the amazing testimonies He created in us and the reconciliation we had with Jesus, the situation changed us to see how much God loves us.

This is a lifelong walk, but by sharing our stories, He makes us stronger in Him, in His will, and the calling to help others. Having faith in His will is what pleases Him and will fill our empty void in our hearts. Like God's Word says again in one of my favorite verses: "Without faith, it is impossible to please Him." Again, I realize where I come from and what God has done in my life, and I was able to forgive and keep forgiving because God has forgiven me of so much.

"Therefore, I tell you, her many sins have been forgiven—as her great love has shown. But whoever has been forgiven little loves little" (Luke 7:47 NIV).

Jesus died on the cross in my place, and seeing him with all my sins upon that cross, who am I not to forgive others, especially my husband? This taught me not to take for granted what Jesus did for me on the precious cross of Calvary. Sometimes, we forget as we age in Christ where he took us out of, and then when things like these happen to us, we are not strong in Him. I am encouraging you to go back to your first encounter of forgiveness, LOVE, and grace you had with God, and ask Him for His love to fill you AGAIN so that you can pour this out to others when they sin against you and hurt you.

Forgiveness and gratitude are the keys to unlock His blessings and His will. To forgive, we need to heal our souls, our hearts, and our minds, and then fill them with His word, His presence, and His love.

(3 John 1:2 NLV)

"Dear friends, I hope all is well with you and that you are as healthy in body as you are strong in spirit." We can't hear from Him when we do not forgive. All you have to care about in this life is to receive His forgiveness so then you can forgive others. Jesus is alive, and he loves you very much. Today, I am encouraging you not to just seek Him once a week but every day! This will help you know the true and this truth of who He and who you are in Him is what will set you free!

I needed to be healed to understand God and hear His voice. God was doing a new thing in both of our hearts. He was making us more loving and gracious to one another.

God is greater than all our regrets, and He will never stop chasing you! He is right here with you! He has always been there for you.

Received this song for you my beautiful reader. As I mentioned before, when we worship we feel so close to Him!

Greater Than All My Regrets (*Tenth Avenue North*)

When the past it comes to haunt me It tells me what I've done It reminds me what's gone wrong When my sins are laid before me My Lord, You take them on Yes, my Lord, You take them on So if I fall and if I fail I will trust your mercy is Greater than all of this And if I bend and if I break I'll trust the hands that hold me are Greater than all my regrets You are greater than all my regrets

You are Greater than all my regrets You are, you are Father, I know I break your heart When I choose my way When I doubt your love But you take me as I am, a child Yeah, you whisper in my ear Let's get up and try again So if I fall and

if I fail I will trust your mercy is Greater than all of this And if I bend and if I break I'll trust the hands that hold me are Greater than all my regrets You are greater than all my regrets You are Greater than all my regrets You are, you are Hallelujah, you are right here with me

Hallelujah, you have always been there Hallelujah, you will never stop chasing me You're chasing me, God Hallelujah, you are right here with me
Hallelujah, you have always been there Hallelujah, you will never stop chasing me You're chasing me So if I fall and if I fail I will trust your mercy is Greater than all of this And if I bend and if I break I'll trust the hands that hold me are Greater than all my regrets Greater than all my regrets You are greater than all my regrets You are Greater than all my

regrets You are, you are!

Source: *Musixmatch*
Songwriters: David Leonard / Mike Donehey / Jeff Owen Greater Than All My Regrets lyrics © Integrity'S Alleluia Music, HYATT STREET PUBLISHING

Chapter Eight

Codependence & How to Heal From It

In this chapter, I will talk about codependency and how I overcame it. My story will be the key that will unlock your prison! One true reality I have shared throughout this book is when we share our stories with others, it allows us to be free and unlock ourselves to let things out of us and then encourage others. When we do this, we start realizing everything that happened to us or will happen to us is because of a purpose, and that purpose was for our healing and freedom. This will help us and others understand and trust God's amazing grace.

It was through opening my heart in sharing my testimony that I was able to find a safe place in my life. Today, I have found encouragement from His Word and His people and more of His healing to continue my life. Our hearts get softer when we share our stories with each other. When we do, we impart and share God's word with love. **(Revelation 12:11)** teaches us: **"And they have defeated him by the blood of the Lamb and by their testimony. And they did not love their lives so much that they were afraid to die."** In my life journey, I have struggled with codependence. I thought I was in control and needed to figure everything out, but it was not the case. I had to repent and start training my mind to let go and let God! I believe this was part of all my sufferings, and I believe we all have struggled with this in our lives at some point.

Codependency refers to a situation in which individuals depend on others to meet their emotional needs; however, it is usually practiced selfishly and could be damaging. This could be a father-mother relationship or husband and wife or child and mother or father and son. In present times, the meaning of codependence has expanded that it now defines various kinds of damaging patterns of relationship. Overall, they are almost the same. The Word of God speaks about codependence:

"The fear of man lays a snare, but whoever trusts in the Lord is safe" *(Proverbs 29:25).*

Pride and arrogance are negative feelings. Since these feelings make people focus on themselves, they blind people, and people cannot even see their true selves and how God sees them.

Though God showers His love on us irrespective of our sins; He also tells us that humans are not perfect; they commit sins and are in need of a true savior every day.

"And Jesus said to him, "Why do you call me good? No one is good except God alone" (Mark 10:18).

Codependent people appear to be very faithful, but this faithfulness causes damaging effects. They support illogically, so they support sinful activities and attitudes too.

We all want others to think so much about us, so most of us try to show a pleasing attitude and make a false appearance that can hide our flaws. People require creating boundaries to keep good opinions about themselves and prevent being a victim of manipulation. But codependent persons find themselves incomplete and try to imitate others or associate with people to seek an identity. In this effort, they lose their ability to make choices on their own since they seek to keep their dependent relationships. Moreover, they start crossing boundaries in a bid to control other people because they do not focus themselves anymore.

Let me reassure you that the bible has solutions to every problem that we face today. I made the bible my source of strength to get rid of being in a codependent relationship because the bible also tells us how we should relate with others.

"And let us consider how to stir up one

another to love and good works, not neglecting to meet together, as is the habit of some, but encouraging one another, and all the more as you see the Day drawing near" (Hebrew 10:24-25).

The interdependence among Christians is highly instrumental in living through Christ and thriving as Christians. To become good Christians, we must avoid selfish desires and start believing in helping each other. The Christian way of life is completely opposite to selfishness, deceit, and harmfulness of codependence and it is found in the following biblical verses:

"A new commandment I give to you, that you love one another: just as I have loved you, you also are to love one another. By this all people will know that you are my disciples, if you have love for one another" *(John 13:34-35).*

"For by the grace given to me I say to everyone among you not to think of himself more highly than he ought to think, but to think with sober judgment, each according to the measure of faith that God has assigned. For as in one body we have many members and the members do not all have the same function, So we, though many, are one body in Christ, and individually members one of another. 6 Having gifts that differ according to thegrace given to us, let us use them: if prophecy, in proportion to our faith"** *(Romans 12:3-6).*

"Do nothing from selfish ambition or conceit, but in humility count others more significant than yourselves. 4 Let each of you look not only to his own interests, but also to the interests of others" *(Philippians 2:3-4).*

For me, to heal of codependence in my marriage, I had to trust and give all my heart to God, who in His Word explains clearly, why I was reacting this way. I learned that programs that helped me in my journey, such as Celebrate Recovery, were a real blessing to me. In these programs, I learned many principles that I now apply every day of my life.

In His word, I have realized that I'm not God. I admit that I am powerless to control my tendency to do the wrong things and that I am powerless over my compulsive behaviors. This reminds me of this bible verse: **"Blessed are the poor in spirit, for theirs is the kingdom of heaven"** (Matthew 5:3).

**"So now it is no longer I who do it, but sin that dwells within me. 18 For I know that nothing good dwells in me, that is, in my flesh. For I have the desire to do what is right, but not the ability to carry it out" *(Romans 7:17-18).*

I've made my decision and believe that God exists, that I matter to Him, and that He has the power to help me. **"Blessed are those who mourn, for they shall be comforted"** *(Matthew 5:4).*

I believe that a power greater than myself could restore me to sanity. **"for it is God who works in you, both to will and to work for his good pleasure"** *(Philippians 2:13).*

I have consciously chosen to commit all my life and will to Christ's care and control. **"Happy are the meek."** *(Matthew 5:5).*

I have openly examined and confessed my faults to myself, to God, and to someone I trust. **"Happy are the pure in heart."** *(Matthew 5:8-3).*

I have made a decision to turn my life and my will over to the care of God. **"I appeal to you therefore, brothers, by the mercies of God, to present your bodies as a living sacrifice, holy and acceptable to God, which is your spiritual worship" (Romans 12:1).**

I have admitted being entirely ready and voluntarily submitted to any changes God wants to make in my life and humbly ask Him to remove my character defects.

"Humble yourselves before the Lord, and he will lift you up" *(James 4:10).*

I have humbly asked Him to remove all my shortcomings. **"If we confess our sins, he is faithful and will forgive us our sins and purify us from all unrighteousness"** (1 John 1:9).

"Happy are those whose greatest desire is to do what God requires" *(Matthew 5:6 4).*

I have made a searching and fearless moral inventory of myself. **"Let us examine our ways and test them, and let us return to the Lord"** *(Lamentations 3:40).*

I have evaluated all of my relationships. I offer forgiveness to those who have hurt me and make amends for harm I've done to others when possible, except when doing so tends to harm them or others. **"Happy are the merciful"** *(Matthew 5:7)* **"Happy are the peacemakers"** (Matthew 5:9).

I have admitted to God, to myself, and to every human being, the exact nature of my wrongs.

"Therefore, confess your sins to each other and pray for each other so that you may be healed." *(James 5:16).*

I have made a list of all persons we had harmed and became willing to make amends to them all. **"Do to others, as you would have them do to you"** *(Luke 6:31).*

I have learned to reserve a daily time with God for self-examination, Bible reading, and prayer in order to know God and His will for my life and to gain the power to follow His will. I have yielded myself to God to be used to bring this Good News to others, both by examples and my words.

"Happy are those who are persecuted because they do what God requires" *(Matthew 5:10).* I have continually taken personal inventory, and when I am wrong, I promptly admit it.

"So, if you think you are standing firm, be careful that you don't fall!" *(1 Corinthians 10:12).*

I seek through prayer and meditation to improve my conscious contact with God, praying only for knowledge of His will for me and power to carry them out.

"Let the word of Christ dwell in you richly" (Colossians 3:16).

Having had a spiritual experience as the result of these steps, I try to carry this message to others and practice these principles in all my affairs.

"Brothers, if someone is caught in a sin, you who are spiritual should restore them gently. But watch yourself, or you also may be tempted" *(Galatians 6:1.)*

These prayers and many others played a key role in my healing, and I wanted to share them all with you, especially, The Serenity Prayer by Reinhold Niebuhr:

"God, give us the grace to accept with serenity
The things that cannot be changed,
Courage to change the things
Which should be changed,
And the Wisdom to distinguish
The one from the other. Living one day at a time,
Enjoying one moment at a time,
Accepting hardship as a pathway to peace,
Taking, as Jesus did,
This sinful world as it is,
Not as I would have it,
Trusting that you will make all things right,

If I surrender to your will,
So that I may be reasonably happy in this life,
And supremely happy with you forever in the next."
In Jesus name, Amen.

I have realized that every testimony, no matter what it is, reveals that we are not alone, and we need each other. Every testimony has power! When we give our lives to Christ, situations do not get better, but we get better! We learn how to go through those situations with His grace and peace. I learned that walking closer to God helped me again to make better choices.

We know that being married is God's will, so we need His grace and mercy every day in our marriages. Every marriage is different, but all marriages require that we fight and pray daily. There are some rare times when God tells us to let a toxic marriage go, for example, an abusive marriage. My situation was clear, and God was calling me to fight and believe and for there to be a breakthrough, and this very testimony you are reading today.

Jesus said, "For those who are forgiven much, love much. I know I've been forgiven a lot. It was easy for me to forgive my husband, not for what he did to me, but rather what Jesus has done for me. When I look back at my past life, I see I was nothing without Him.

Those days I was hurt, lost, broken, and with no direction, but when I met Jesus, he simply filled every empty hole in my heart and my life. He guided me with His word and I understood what real love was. So, forgiving others was easy for me, based on a deep inventory of what God has forgiven me of already.

We need to believe that He will pour on us, His grace, and be merciful to every situation. We are called to pray and fight for our marriage, but sometimes God calls us to let go. He does not like this option because everyone is affected, but sometimes for Him to work; it has to happen. This was not my case! God needed to work in both of us so that we could enjoy one another as He intended too.

Always remember forgiveness is a powerful instrument to make your life happy, and it is the opposite of what Satan wants. He wants us to keep hurting and keep feeling the pain so that we can keep hurting others.

That is why **(Romans 12:21)** says, **"Don't let evil conquer you, but conquer evil by doing good."** So, when you forgive, you are doing the ultimate good. This is what the cross of Christ is all about. It's where Satan is defeated every day.

When you forgive, you are sowing a seed of goodness into the ground, and that is your life. That seed will always grow up to bear good fruit. It simply requires faith. As God's word says, **"Without faith, it is impossible to please God."** Our walk with Jesus is all about faith. Faith that God is who He says He is, and by obeying Him, you will see the fruits, though sometimes not right away. But like any good tree, it takes time to grow.

"And let us not grow weary of doing good, for in due season we will reap, if we do not give up" (Galatians 6:9).

Are you ready for your harvest? You are if you have been sowing good seed in faith and obedience to God. Often, we can either grow bitter or better with God. It all depends on what we do with the hurt the world has given us. We all have it, no matter what family or neighborhood you grew up in because we are all born into sin. Nobody is born better than anyone else in terms of sin. We all have been affected by it in one way or another. The key is, "what do we do with that sin, hurt and shame? Some use it as an excuse for more acts of sin. Others blame society. Some blame family and spouses. The fact remains, as stated in **(Ephesians 6:12):**

"For we do not wrestle against flesh and blood, but against the rulers, against the authorities, against the cosmic powers over this present darkness, against the spiritual forces of

evil in the heavenly places."

When we know who the true enemy is, we can fight against it. When we realize that our enemy is not our family or spouse, we can formulate an effective plan of attack. Our lives and testimonies should be the fuel and motivation for us to fight the good fight of faith. With the grace of God in our lives, our lives turn into beautiful, green luscious trees in the desert, not dry ones in the desert. **(Hebrews 12:15)** says:

"See to it that no one fails to obtain the grace of God; that no "root of bitterness" springs up and causes trouble, and by it many become defiled."

You can see to it that no one falls short of the grace of God and that no bitter root grows up to cause trouble and defile many. See how important God's grace is in our lives every day. When we forgive others, we receive that grace in our lives. It is like water for our garden in a dry and weary land. In Isaiah, God talks about the coming of Messiah, who will bring rivers to our dry and desolate lives.

"Behold, I am doing a new thing; now it springs forth, do you not perceive it? I will make a way in the wilderness and rivers in the desert. The

wild beasts will honor me, the jackals and the ostriches, for I give water in the wilderness, rivers in the desert, to give drink to my chosen people, the people whom I formed for myself that they might declare my praise" (Isaiah 43:19-21).

This is how we turn our lives from bitter to better with the grace of God in our lives. It is simple, and it is about receiving it ourselves every day so that we can give that grace to others around us who need it. See, life is all about seasons, also different ones, and this is for every single soul in this world, and this is what makes it fun and challenging.

Yes, God knows all things, and He wanted to prepare me for what I was about to experience in this broken world. He wanted to prepare me to understand, forgive, and love two broken souls that thought they were healed, but no He still needed to do a bigger work; those two wretched souls were my husband and me.

For me, my codependence didn't allow me to love as God loves, to see as God sees, and act like God wanted me to act. I recovered from control and trying to fix things and letting go. I learned how to trust Jesus and his words, the more. I recovered from worrying because my mind was never in peace. I learned what God teaches us in

(Philippians 4:8):

"Finally, brothers, whatever is true, whatever is honorable, whatever is just, whatever is pure, whatever is lovely, whatever is commendable, if there is any excellence, if there is anything worthy of praise, think about these things."

I learned not to lean on my own understanding of Him but to trust Him fully. Having support helps and doing His will every day through listening to His words and seeing the right things helped me to be persistent, to be obedient, and to have more faith. It also helped me keep my job stable and think better and not meditating on negative things, but on good things.

By seeking Him, today, I can tell you that all His promises are real, and He truly rewards those who diligently seek Him. He is rewarding you because you are seeking Him right now just by reading this book!

I recovered from insecurities when I allowed the love of God to fill me so that I would hear from Him and let Him work in my husband, while he was working in me. This helped me! Now, emotions of fear and anger have less control over me because I have decided to give Him everything and praised Him in any circumstances every day!

Trying to control and change someone is a difficult thing to do. It is so exhausting! God is the only one who can change people, and He has plans for everyone. All we can change is ourselves. So, be more patient, loving, and compassionate. He also showed me that this walk is not about me, but His work in me. I learned that it is the goodness of God that leads us to repentance.

"Or do you presume on the riches of his kindness and forbearance and patience, not knowing that God's kindness is meant to lead you to repentance?" (Romans 2:4).

I learned not to expect someone else's good behaviors or intentions but to trust God and expect only from Him. I learned that whatever happens in my life is good. Everything is for me to give glory to Him to grow, no matter what it is, as long as I am honoring Him at all times. He will always work it out for good.

I defeated fear because fear is the opposite of faith. If I seek Him every day, faith will increase and prepare me for times when life Satan or my emotions kick on me or sets traps on me.

I learned that protecting my eyes from what I see, my ears from what I hear, my hands from what they touch, and my feet from where they go, I can overcome half of my fears and temptations. I learned that guarding my heart and my mind, is a must for my growth. Hearing music that edifies me is what fills me and bring me closer to Him.

I learned that with God's word and the right heart, I can fight any situation, and we must fight any situation with the truth until the day we see Jesus face to face. If things don't work in your timing, they will definitely work in His timing. When we realize that this life is all about us being sanctified and perfected to see Him, we will understand the purpose of our calling and why we are going through our circumstances.

I learned that it is much better to be transparent with God about our sins and struggles this will make our hearts pure and we will start understanding that no sin is bigger than others; every sin, small or big, is a sin in God's eyes. The joy of the Lord is our strength, knowing Him gives us joy, peace every single day.

At times, we think that because we are closer to God, everything will work in our favor. But I have learned, even as Christians, we will encounter many tests and many situations where we are going to be hurt, or we are going to hurt others.

Why so?

This is because we are all growing into

maturity in Him until the "Day" we see Him face to face, and that is the reason we are all here on earth right now. While I was writing this book, His words were brought out, and this is beautiful because sometimes we don't know how much of His Word we have in our hearts until we write them down. All I know is that His timing is perfect. When you trust Him again, He indeed works faster. When you focus on your problems first, when you let Him heal you first, He will solve the problem in the person or situation you are praying for. Knowing His word helped me understand all things work together for good for those who love Him. It is always better to let go and to let God enter. When you are closer to Him, He prepares you for battle, and when you are focused on Him, He will restore your problem faster, and He will restore the years that you thought you lost.

There is a sense of hope and security that if we do our part and believe it, the chances are that our situations will be better. Sharing all these bible verses in my own book helps me grow writing helps me grow! I want you to cheerfully guard these bible verses in your heart and mind because they are a necessity when we go through tough, good, and bad times in our lives.

Let's review some awesome verses again to take them to heart;

"Trust in the Lord with all your heart and lean not on your own understanding; in all your ways submit to him, and he will make your paths straight. This reminds me to walk by faith and not by sight; we have to truly trust him"(Proverbs 3: 5-6).

"He says, "Be still, and know that I am God" (Psalm 46:10).

This, for me, means when we are still, we can hear from Him clearly, and we will not make emotional decisions but His will.

"As for you Satan, you meant evil against me, but God meant it for good, to bring it about that many people should be kept alive, as they are today" (Genesis 50:20).

See, anything bad that comes to your life is not God's will, but He allows it to happen for your growth and because we live in a world filled with hurt.

"No temptation has overtaken you that is not common to man. God is faithful, and he will not let you be tempted beyond your ability, but with the temptation he will also provide the way of escape, that you may be able to endure it." (1 Corinthians 10:13).

This gives us hope!

"And let us consider how to stir up one another to love and good works, not neglecting to meet together, as is the habit of some, but encouraging one another, and all the more as you see the Day drawing near" (Hebrews 10:24-25).

This verse always spoke to me about accountability and getting together to be encouraged to love and to be comforted by others. It is when He prepared me for what I was about to experience. This means it is a must that you do not isolate yourself when you are going through problems or when you are not going through problems. It also means that we should obey His Words in this verse, always!

"But seek first the kingdom of God and his righteousness, and all these things will be added to you" (Matthew 6:33 33).

This verse helped me to do the right thing; thus, even in my hurt and confusion, I was obedient to do what was right not to cheat, or to get depressed; not to revenge or use my situation in exchange of a sin that could make me feel better but just for a few minutes. Because that's what sin is, it just makes you feel good for a season but then you are empty again. I seek Him by listening to music that heals me, by going out with people who edify me, by working hard and not giving up on my own life.

Today, I understand many with their struggles because I went through them also. Now I can be able to love and help others when they are having marriage problems because I went through them, I can also help a teenager or women who has done wrong choices like for example an abortion and guide her through her healing because I was once there. Just understanding the pain of losing a loved one breaks my heart but because I had two loses, I can help guide and direct many that have experienced this and direct them to Him, The author and perfecter of our faith. I can also now relate to girls who struggle with insecurities with fear and low self-esteem because I was or I am still one of them. This shows me this walk is real and when we all reach the top of our mountain and heal from it, we can be free and enjoy our lives like the Lord intended for us to enjoy from the inside out! Charm is deceitful and beauty is passing but a women who fears the Lord shall be praised! Freedom and submission to God and His presence is all we need to be able to be liberated. We all need each other, so let's continue to love and heal ourselves so we can be able to love our neighbor as ourselves. Neighbor means EVERYONE we come in contact with!

When we get filled with Him we can empty

ourselves by giving to others! This should be our daily Godly routine to be a happy soul.

Epilogue

To all my readers, I want to say that your soul is the most valuable treasure among all things in this world. As a mother or a father, you are supposed to ensure the souls of the people under your care; your children, husband, parents, and siblings are saved. It is the most satisfying thought that you will meet your loved ones again in eternity. Apart from knowing they will go to heaven when they pass, you will also be at peace knowing that they will grow up to fear and love God in this dark generation and understand the difference between what is true and false pure or impure and make a difference. See, you want your child to be a leader not a follower. I see people that try their best to bring their children all kinds of material things, or all sorts of knowledge and education and this is ok, but this is not something that can help them receive salvation. I don't ask you to stop fulfilling their desires altogether, not a long shot. Just be aware of offering them a balance physical mental and spiritual life. As a parent, it is also your job, and the best job actually, to teach them the Word of God and help them understand and encourage their purpose in their life. This is what is going to really fill them. Every sin or mistake or wrong choice they make is in God's hands your job is to teach them God's word and His love for them. Down below is a prayer you can use to invite your loved ones to get to know Jesus in a more personal way.

The sinner's prayer is a prayer a person prays to God when they understand that they are a sinner and in need of a Savior. Saying a sinner's prayer will not accomplish anything on its own. A true sinner's prayer only represents what a person knows, understands, and believes about their sinfulness and need for salvation. Saying the sinner's prayer is simply a way of declaring to God that you are relying on Jesus Christ as your Savior. **(Romans 10:9 NIV)** explains:

"If you declare with your mouth, "Jesus is Lord," and believe in your heart that God raised him from the dead, you will be saved."

There are no "magical" words that result in salvation. It is only faith in Jesus' death and resurrection that can save us. If you understand that you are a sinner and in need of salvation through Jesus Christ, here is a sinner's prayer you can pray to God:

"God, I know that I am a sinner. I know

that I deserve the consequences of my sin. However, I am trusting in Jesus Christ as my Savior. I believe that His death and resurrection provided for my forgiveness. I trust in Jesus and Jesus alone as my personal Lord and Savior. Thank you Lord, for saving me and forgiving me! Amen!"

Whatever we hear and see, affect everything in our life, our faith, our beliefs, our morality, our decisions, our actions, our words, our minds, and our hearts; basically, everything in life, the way you think and act, your emotions, your words, your decisions, your behavior.

If we don't exercise the fruit of the spirit, which is self-control, if we cannot invite God, and His spirit because there is no reverence fear of God, it is very difficult to discipline our minds. This temporary mind needs to be filled with eternal things and that is His Word! To some people, this may mean saying no to violent games or negative TV shows that have strange behaviors — saying no to what is impure, what is rude, and to what is not praiseworthy.

See, what is in your heart and mind is what you are going to give to others. This depends on how you are going to treat people, how you are going to forgive people of offenses, and how you will love them. The more positive, encouraging, and loving things you watch or hear, the more you will become like Him. Yes, we can see and hear other stuff that will distract us from Him, but it will all be temporary, and will NOT reach the soul. I am talking about guarding our hearts and balancing our lives. When we watch a movie that has lots of curses, or acts of violence, they invoke negativity and take us away from God.

The best fellowship we can have with our kids, which are truly meaningful and eternal, are sharing God's word. We need to be careful who is feeding them spiritually; it's either going to be the world or us.

Our hearts are naturally hard, and they get harder because of sin and wrong choices. What God does when He comes in our hearts is soften our hard hearts. Also, sin passes through our previous generations, and we tend to be arrogant and selfish. That's why starting to teach our kids about Him at an early age is very important.

For those who were not believers when they grew up, what they heard and saw formed them to what they are now. For those who were believers and departed from the truth, God promises to bring them back again if you were obedient to this truth of teaching them God's Word at an early age! Isn't this the best promise!

People or kids who killed meditated on the wrong things all their lives, and they did not receive encouragement or love from their parents or those around them. They never guard their hearts and protected their minds. This caused depression, aimlessness, anger, and mental diseases. Meditating on the wrong things causes your mind to deteriorate and act upon evil, dangerous things that will make you do bad choices.

Listening and watching the right things every day have helped me love others the way God wants me to love them, defend my faith the way I need to and lead others to the power, love, and knowledge of God.

Our prayers every day need to be asking God to fill our hearts with His love, to have Him present in our lives at all times. Loving people, accepting them just where they are! More of Him and less of me, less of my own selfish desires. It is a process, but the beauty of this walk is that God does not accept perfect people, we do not have to be perfect to please God, the opposite He uses broken people all the time and we are all broken and in need of Him. The beauty of this walk is that He makes us righteous! Jesus makes us good in Gods eyes! It is not our works; we are saved by grace and faith alone in Him!

God's promises come through faith and patience. We need to realize that our children can't spend their time with desires that will bring worldly joys only. We must inspire our children to recognize God regularly by teaching them the Word of God. Let us follow God's commandments with peace and joy. I can assure you this will bring peace and comfort to you.

I spend my time with peace as I celebrate my salvation in Christ. I thank God for His blessings. Every good thing that comes to us is because of His grace. We should encourage others to turn to God every day. We never know when the end of that person's life will come. With Christ's love and hope, we will always live as if it is our last day in this world. Let us smile and rejoice for His forgiveness, His Word, and our salvation in Christ with every breath we take. Let God open your heart to know Him through His Word every day. Glorify Him everywhere you go! Be creative in sharing His love and Word! I assure your life will be filled with his desires and his unique joy, and love. Worship God every day, protect your eyes, and choose wisely whatever you hear and see. In my 15-year walk with Him, I have guarded my heart, and this is one thing that has healed me, and it will heal you all too! This will definitely bring stability and purpose.

I would like to end this book with these

biblical verses that are dear to my heart; it is quite an honor and good news for us, which is from Jesus because we have not seen him as the apostles did. We need to know that God only wants us to have faith just like a mustard seed! This seed is the smallest of all seeds and that's all we need to believe! Like a child, we need to start, continue, and end our journey of faith in Him. Keep on encouraging one another and loving one another because it is what we all need until the last breath of our lives!

To all my readers' gratitude will be the biggest and strongest word I can use to end this book I never underestimate or take for granted every day. Why? Because sometimes we say, every day is a gift, but we do not really believe it because we are stuck in the temporary problems or wonders of this world. Worry, anxiety will not change anything about your problems not a bit! But something that will change your perspective about your problem is being grateful. Trust me, if anything stays in your heart about this book you are reading, let it be gratitude! Start by thanking Him every day for absolutely everything and you will see a change in your heart and mind. This is then when things will change and all your problems will get better in your life.

Thanking God every day for my health, my mind, and my emotional stability; focusing on the things I have and not on the things I do not have is necessary in our life journey. Again, God mentions this in His word, He said thanking Him before you see things happen is also called faith! Without faith is impossible to please Him! See His love towards us is unconditional. You do not have to do anything because He already did everything for you! Seeking Him is the secrete to know Him and understand what He wants us to do in any circumstance.

"Then Jesus told him, "You believe because you have seen me. Blessed are those who believe without seeing me" (John 20:29).

"Do you think anyone is going to be able to drive a wedge between us and Christ's love for us? There is no way! Not trouble, not hard times, not hatred, not hunger, not homelessness, not bullying threats, not backstabbing, not even the worst sins listed in Scripture: None of this fazes us because Jesus loves us. I'm absolutely convinced that nothing—nothing living or dead, angelic or demonic, today or tomorrow, high or low, thinkable or unthinkable—absolutely nothing can get between us and God's love because of the way that Jesus our Master has embraced us." (Romans 8:31-39 MSG),

To end, He also assures us about His Love again in his precious Word:

(Ephesians 3:18 MSG)

"God can do anything, you know—far more than you could ever imagine, guess, or request in your wildest dreams! He does it not by pushing us around but by working within us, his Spirit deeply and gently within us."

References

Celebrate recovery

Gotquestions.org

Wikipedia

NLT Bible

NKJ Bible

Father's Love Letter used by permission
Father Heart Communications
©1999 FathersLoveLetter.com

www.ingramcontent.com/pod-product-compliance
Lightning Source LLC
LaVergne TN
LVHW021306150425
808708LV00003B/36